The Laws of the Web

The Laws of the Web

Patterns in the Ecology of Information

Bernardo A. Huberman

The MIT Press
Cambridge, Massachusetts
London, England

This book was set in Palatino by The MIT Press.

Printed and bound in the United States of America.

Library of Congress Cataloging-in-Publication Data

Huberman, B. A. (Bernardo A.), 1943–
    The laws of the Web : patterns in the ecology of information / Bernardo A. Huberman.
        p. cm.
    Includes bibliographical references (p.   ).
    ISBN 0-262-08303-5 (alk. paper)
        1. Internet searching. 2. World Wide Web—Social aspects. I. Title.
    ZA4226 .H83 2001
    025.04—dc21   2001032621

Contents

Preface

In a short period of time the World Wide Web has become not only the de facto information medium for hundreds of millions of individuals, but also an object of keen interest to a number of scientists intrigued by its enormity, complexity, and global reach. This interest stems from the fact that in spite of its haphazard growth the Web hides powerful underlying regularities: from the way its link structure is organized to the patterns that one finds in its use by millions of people. To detect and explain these regularities is now part of an ongoing effort in a number of laboratories, and while the activity is partly explanatory, it has practical implications. It does not escape those engaged in this search that this new knowledge can be used in the design of novel mechanisms with great potential for increased efficiency in the use of the Web for a myriad of purposes.

The discovery of several regularities has already shed light on how information is stored and linked within the Web, how individuals use it, and how people interact on a massive scale when foraging for information in this new medium. Some of these results were established through the use of standard online surveys, not unlike those deployed in other social domains. Other studies rely on well-known methodologies in statistics and economics. But what makes part of this effort interesting is that many of these regularities or laws have been predicted on the basis of theoretical models adopted from a field of physics, statistical mechanics, which few would have thought were applicable to the social domain.

For the past thirteen years, I have applied methods from statistical mechanics and nonlinear dynamics to the study of large distributed systems, ranging from economic systems to the Internet at large. The effort, made in collaboration with a small group of people, led to a number of powerful insights and interesting applications that unfortunately escaped wide attention because of the technical language in which they were couched. And yet, a number of people who saw beyond the mathematical formalism of our work urged me over the years to put in the effort needed to explain the power of this methodology to a nontechnical audience.

This book is an attempt to do precisely that, using the Web as the focus of those methods. The Web is so ubiquitous and accessible that it provides both a subject familiar to most people and a unique laboratory for the study of its growth and structure. But unfortunately, the ease with which it can be studied does not facilitate the translation of concepts couched in mathematical equation into plain language. However, since I firmly believe that concepts from any field should be easily explained in plain language, I have tried to convey the main ideas using simple examples and resorting to experiences that most of us encounter in everyday life.

In doing so, I'm aware of the fact that the technical-minded reader might wince at apparently long explanations that could be compressed into a couple of equations, or smile condescendingly at the amount of detail swept under the rug for the sake of clarity of transmission. By way of apology I state that I know of no better way to convey the flavor and power of these laws to a reader's attention without asking him or her for a long investment in learning a number of technical fields. More important, I believe that while the search and explanation of these laws involve a certain technical sophistication, their import and consequences are within the grasp of anyone interested enough in the subject. A long experience in giving talks on this subject to very diverse audiences has taught me that questions and comments from lay members of the audience are a continuous source of ideas and challenges for the continuation of my work.

The first suggestion to write a book about these methods, addressed to a nontechnical audience, was made to me by Baldo Faieta, an early fan of this approach. However tempting his arguments, I balked at the sheer effort to produce a coherent story with enough focus to keep the attention of the reader. Later on, a number of people—notably Scott Clearwater, Eytan Adar, Natalie Glance, my wife Mette, my children Lara and Andrew, Mark Lurie, and Christoph Loch—insisted on the potential value of such a book while providing a vague assurance that they could be counted among those who might read it. Finally, under the gentle and persuasive prodding of Bob Prior of The MIT Press, I started writing it in Paris, France, while visiting INSEAD, the European School of Business. A number of lectures and discussions with colleagues in that school helped me refine some of the arguments, while earlier papers written for popular journals with Natalie Glance and Lada Adamic taught me how to articulate in plain English arguments that had previously been couched in technical jargon.

While the effort and responsibility for this book are mine, its contents are the result of a long collaboration with a number of colleagues and students without whom I would have little to say. Tad Hogg has been a fellow traveler in many aspects of this enterprise from the beginning. Natalie Glance, Rajan Lukose, Lada Adamic, Eytan Adar, Jim Pitkow, Sebastian Maurer, Matt Franklin, Alessandro Acquisti, Peter Pirolli, and Amit Puniyani were instrumental in making the research successful and in sharing with me their insights and excitement. Per-Kristian Halvorsen saw to it that the work described here was supported. Finally, Sebastian Doniach prodded me to explain each new result with the healthy skepticism of a true academic.

This book could not have been finished without supportive and objective readers able to comment on its contents and style while suggesting needed improvements. I thank Bob Prior for playing his true editor's role, and my loving gratitude goes to Mette for proofreading the manuscript, for telling me what needed to be changed, and most important, for understanding what it took to write it.

Palo Alto, January 2001

1   E-cology

In a small building in the picturesque Presidio area of the city of San Francisco, a group of people engages in the twenty-first century equivalent of a giant ecological survey without even having to leave their desks. Using workstations programmed to crawl the vast expanses of the Internet, workers at the Internet Archive continuously retrieve and store for future study the entire textual content of the World Wide Web, from sites in the Silicon Valley to remote servers on the other side of the earth. In a sense they are not only acting as ecologists but constructing a library that will soon dwarf the largest libraries of the world, such as the Library of Congress or the French Bibliothèque Nationale. As of July 2000, they had collected one billion Web pages, which amounts to 33.5 terabytes, and the collection keeps growing at a rate of 10 percent a month. To get an idea of the size of this collection, consider that a book contains about a megabyte of data, and a terabyte is a million megabytes. The size of the Library of Congress of the United States, which contains twenty million books, is therefore twenty terabytes (not counting pictures).

While the size of the Web and the pace of its growth are staggering, its contents don't need to be housed in a large building. Unlike venerable institutions such as the American

Museum of Natural History in New York or the British Museum in London, the Internet Archive project houses the entire collection in a storage server the size of a refrigerator. It is not clear how big the full archive will eventually be, or how much of what is today on the Web will persist in a few years. The object of this activity is to preserve for future study this transient data embedded in a permanent medium—studies that they feel will be of interest to scientists, historians, and journalists. And to access the data, there is no need to take a trip to such a beautiful setting, for it can be browsed from any computer in the world with the proper authorization.

Welcome to the Information Age, an age of instant access to the most diverse and arcane knowledge at almost no cost, and where electronic signals are starting to replace in value the bulky manufactured goods that used to define the wealth of nations, companies, and individuals. And this is just the beginning. Impressed as we are with what we now see, in a few years it will seem quaint and outdated when compared to the wonders that cyberspace will bring to most people on this earth.

The workers at the Internet Archive are not alone. On the opposite side of the United States, a group of researchers in the Computer Science Department at Boston University engage in an activity that in some ways complements that of the Internet Archive. By instrumenting a number of Web browsers so that they can track which specific sites users visit and how long they stay on particular pages, they try to establish patterns of use that can lead to an understanding of information foraging on the Web, and thus better designs for Web servers. They are another example of scientists starting to address the content and the structure of the Web with the same keen interest biologists bring to their study of the tropical rainforest. Move down to New Jersey, and one finds researchers at the Nippon Electric Company (NEC) laboratories in Princeton sampling the content of the Web in order to establish its size and determine how much of it eventually ends up listed by the search engines that most people use. Not much, it turns out.

Back in California and a few miles south of the Presidio area, in the hills surrounding Stanford University, scientists at the Internet Research Group of the Xerox Palo Alto Research Center have been poking and analyzing the vast repository of the Web. Their work, which uses the data that is collected by the Internet Archive and many other sources, has uncovered in the past three years a number of hidden patterns within the Web that hold clues as to how people interact in cyberspace and forage for information. These patterns, and those found by other researchers, are both surprising and interesting. We have already established, for example, that the distribution of pages and links per Web site follows a universal and lawful behavior, with few sites having enormous numbers of pages and many having a few. Or that the congestion created by surfers on the Web gives rise to predictable Internet "storms" that suddenly appear and subside in statistically meaningful patterns.

The reason these results are surprising is that no one would have anticipated finding anything regular when considering the chaotic fashion in which the Web grows. No central planner tells its users how to design their sites, forage for information, or even how to organize the links that allow for users to surf from one page or site to another. The structure and content of the Web is the result of actions by millions of people who seldom, if ever, think of the global implications of adding an extra page or a link to their sites. Thus, it is natural to expect that studies of the Internet can only uncover a very random and featureless Web instead of the lawful behavior they find.

Another aspect of these strong regularities exists that makes them interesting, and it has to do with their origins, which in turn relates to the way they are explained. Rather than just exploiting these regular patterns in the design of better sites or strategies for dealing with congestion, they can also be explained by theories that take into account the detailed behavioral mechanisms of Web users and designers of sites. As the theories then proceed to connect the individual level to the aggregate behavior of the Web, they shed light on a number of social mechanisms that are operational beyond the World Wide Web. Examples of such insights are provided by laws that explain how people surf, how they interact with one another through congestion patterns, and how they determine the popularity of given sites. From this perspective, the Web becomes a gigantic informational ecosystem that can be used to quantitatively measure and test theories of human behavior and social interaction.

In this book, I intend to provide a description of the laws of the Web, along with their implications for the understanding of certain social phenomena and the design of better mechanisms for accessing information. While doing so, I also want to explain the methodology by which these theories are derived, for it offers a novel way of addressing complex problems in social dynamics. While the theories in their original form tend to be cast in a mathematical formalism that allows for precise predictions, the main ideas can be explained in plain words, thus making them accessible to a large audience.

In deriving these laws, I hope also to illustrate a type of approach that has proven successful at explaining the interactions between the local properties or actions of individuals and the collective outcome of their interactions. This approach was initially developed by physicists in order to understand the behavior of matter as a collection of atoms and molecules. While it would be naïve to expect it to be of any use in the context of humans foraging for information, it can be modified by introducing notions of expectations, utility, and rationality on the part of the users. It is only then that one has hope of producing reasonable explanations of human behavior and making predictions that can be tested by measurements on the Web.

Expectations in themselves are important, for humans and many other animals differ from rocks and molecules in that they take into account the future when deciding a particular course of action. The more complex the memory structure of an organism, the further the reach of the horizon that such an entity can take into account. And this means that any study of dynamical behavior involving individuals has to explicitly take into account the projections that we all make about future events, however incorrect they may be.

Each of those laws, from the distribution of pages and links per site to Internet storms, from surfing patterns to the nature of markets, offers a number of insights that are not only interesting in themselves but also beneficial to both providers and consumers. Such insights make access to information more timely and reliable, and they help design better Web sites that incorporate knowledge of surfing patterns by visitors.

In the following chapters I describe some of the hidden laws that govern the growth, structure, and linkage of the Web, and then move on to see how the Internet can be used to understand the interactions among the users that it mediates. I show how congestion can be understood in terms of dilemmas that users face, and how knowledge about the inevitable Internet storms that pepper traffic and slow it down can be used to design faster ways of accessing Web sites. I also point out how surfing exhibits regular patterns that uncover how people forage for information, and how to turn these insights into better design sites. Likewise, I hope to convey a sense of the scale and methodology that we are using to study the social dynamics underpinning the phenomenon of the Internet, for they offer a whole new way of studying social behavior in the Information Age.

2   The Phenomenon of the Web

We are in the midst of a profound transformation whose effects are felt by an increasing fraction of the world's population. Just as the introduction of the steam engine a century and a half ago changed the way people worked and thought of themselves, we are once again undergoing a change whose consequences cannot yet be discerned with clarity. But while the end of this revolution cannot be seen, the change itself is clearly defined. It consists of the replacement of an economy based on the manufacture of physical goods with one whose output is weightless and that has global reach.

For over a hundred years we conceived of industrial production as the transformation of raw materials into physical products, such as machines, tools and devices, which require much energy to create and distribute. From automobiles and television sets to construction work, the assembly and use of such objects has always required large investments of physical energy (most often in the form of heat) and capital, in addition to the design of complex manufacturing and distribution organizations. This process, which we sometimes think of as a rather permanent component of our society, started around 1845 as steam, steel, and railroads started to change the economies of Europe and the United States. By the

turn of the twentieth century a new industrial wave, characterized by the production of electricity, chemicals, and cars
with internal combustion engines, appeared only to be fol-
lowed in the 1950s by another big wave, made up of electronics, aviation, and petrochemicals. Each of these waves
brought changes to the workforce and capital markets, while
shifting the location of wealth to different parts of the world.
This process has been so powerful and relentless in its
unfolding that for much of the twentieth century the world
learned to think of the industrial might of nations in terms of
smokestacks, railroads, and air transportation systems.

This is all changing very fast. For the past few years an
economy of services, consisting of information goods—
including insurance policies, market activities, venture capital, and so forth—has been growing at a very fast pace. This
knowledge-based economy is starting to surpass the traditional, industrial one, in terms of jobs, wealth generated, and
innovation. The numbers in the United States alone paint an
incredible picture. According to a recent Commerce Department report, information technology generated at least a
third of the U.S. economic growth between 1995 and 1998.
During that period, the gross domestic product rose 22 percent, to $8.7 trillion. And because these goods and services
keep getting cheaper, they allow business to become more
productive, cutting inflation while sustaining growth in the
overall economy. Equally important, for the past few years
workers in the new information technologies have been at
least twice as productive as those in the traditional economic
sector such as manufacturing. And since they also earn
almost 80 percent more than other workers, this is bound to
influence young people as they start thinking of what to
engage in as they enter the workforce. Equally impressive, the
report claims that almost half of the American workforce will

be employed in technology-related companies or companies that rely on technology by the year 2006.

These sweeping changes are bound to continue as more industries and individuals perceive the value of engaging in this kind of commerce. As they switch to novel ways of providing services over the Internet to both established business and a gigantic consumer base, they'll continue to create an electronic blanket that will eventually cover and engage us in one form or another. The phenomenon of the Internet start-up company is a manifestation of the enthusiasm with which young people in the United States, Europe, and parts of Latin America jumped into the new economy. Although perhaps known to most readers, the success stories of Yahoo!, Amazon, and eBay act as beacons that attract entrepreneurs and investors willing to risk efforts and capital in exchange for the promise of wealth and community recognition. As with other great economic shifts, it is the young people who seem more willing to engage in this new economy, both because of its high risk and also because of a new cultural phenomenon that confers high status to membership in a start-up. Just as the hippie movement that first started in the United States attracted from all over the world countless numbers of young people in the 1960s and 1970s, start-up activity seemed to convey the same sense of belonging to a transformational wave.

In light of these changes, some people argue that the emergence of this economy based on bits rather than mass will make the present laws of economics irrelevant, as they were developed to explain mechanisms of resource allocation and production suitable to the smokestack industrial age. Moreover, they argue for a new set of economic laws to describe the massless economy, laws that have not yet been clearly articulated. Interestingly, this argument was also made at the start of the twenty-first century when telephony started spreading throughout the United States and the rest of the world. But while the arrival of the massless economy is indeed mediated by a shift in the technology base of most advanced countries, it is not evident that economic laws will become obsolete. Quite the opposite is true. It might be that efficiencies that result from the global reach of information and the removal of many inefficiencies by the new medium provided by the Internet make traditional economics have a wider application to the Information Age than to some aspects of the Industrial Age. One example of this phenomenon is the fact that information, which used to be scarce and thus valuable, is now pervasive, easily reproducible and obtainable through a couple of clicks in a Web browser. As a result almost nothing can be charged for it. If one thinks of real-time stock quotes, which a couple of years ago were available only to traders and market analysts, one realizes the fundamental change the Web has produced. To obtain real-time data it was necessary either to have costly access to an exchange or to subscribe for a considerable amount of money to a service that would provide such data. Today Yahoo! and others offer free access to stock quotes, along with analysts' recommendations and news items related to the company whose stock one wants to find out about. This point has been argued persuasively by a number of economists. Two of them, Shapiro and Varian (1999), have recently shown how standard economic models suffice to explain most of the basic market forces underlying the emergent Information Age.

Since I've already mentioned the coming of the Information Age, it is useful to explain how it came about and what forces mediated the change away from an economy of mass and heat production to a massless one.

Two revolutions are at the heart of the transformation of our society into an Information Age. The first one is in telecommunications, and its roots are technological, political, and economical. That it constitutes a revolution can be appreciated when one considers the cost of sending voice and data over long distances. Whereas a three-minute telephone call from New York to London in 1934 cost $300 in 1996 dollars, today it costs less than a dollar. If this trend continues, it will essentially be free to communicate by voice from one end of the planet to the other. Moreover, data in the form of digital bits has replaced voice as the main consumer of bandwidth. The cost of transmitting data will become a negligible fraction of what it costs to create it. We might even reach a point when sending data over the Internet might be offered for free in exchange for subscriptions to Internet services such as financial investments, health care, home monitoring, and so forth.

The second revolution is the explosive increase in the availability and power of computers over the past twenty years. Moore's Law, named after Intel co-founder Gordon Moore, who came up with the formulation more than three decades ago, states that silicon chips double in complexity every two years. Since chips power computers, DVD players, video cameras, and just about every other electronic gadget imaginable, the implication of Moore's Law is that we'll keep seeing smaller, cheaper, and faster computers and appliances for many years to come. Computers will not be restricted to the familiar box with a screen on top of it. They will be embedded in all sorts of systems, notably cellular telephones and handheld devices, which will enable instant access to remote documents and information from any point on earth.

These two revolutions, one in communications and the other in computational power, made possible the creation of the Internet and the immense connectivity that it implies for people all over the world. Citizens of virtually any country can have, with the click of a mouse, access to timely information and services that not long ago used to be restricted to a few privileged individuals. A striking example of this phenomenon is seen in the new ways by which the scientific community communicates new results. Not long ago, few scientists were fortunate enough to be part of some inner circle that sent to each other advance notice of breakthroughs and new results in their field that would later appear in print. The rest of the scientific community had to wait to learn of new results and discoveries through the mailing of reports and papers, or, more generally but even slower, their publication in scientific journals. This created a class system in science, which was largely defined by who had access to timely information. All this has changed with the advent of the Internet. Now any scientist with access to a computer and the network can instantaneously receive new results and ideas and can contribute to their spread throughout the community. Equally important, access to data that used to be hard to obtain, such as results from large experiments or reprints of papers published in costly journals is now available for free through a number of reliable sources. Thus information, which used to be scarce and therefore expensive, is now plentiful and nearly free, while the scarce resource—and therefore the expensive one— is the knowledge required to process that information.

The example I just gave of the scientific community is not unique, since universal access to information is rapidly spreading to all sorts of people and occupations. Witness the recent surge in popularity of online trading of financial stocks and securities, with millions of people having direct access to financial data from the markets and making investments without resorting to intermediaries that traditionally were the only ones with access to the data. Or the travel industry, once run by agents who had access to airline schedules and pricing, which are now within a mouse click of any potential traveler. The list can go on, and will go on, as entrepreneurial people who see the possibility of starting new business to exploit this very connectivity implement more innovative uses of the medium.

Riding on top of this information revolution mediated by the Internet and further accelerating the advent of the massless economy, is the phenomenon of the World Wide Web. Originally conceived in a physics laboratory in Geneva as a mechanism for distributing information among physicists trying to unravel the ultimate structure of matter, the Web quickly spread worldwide to all sorts of people and business, making it the de facto interactive medium of the Information Age. This spread is nothing but phenomenal. From a few sites available in 1993 to several million in 1998, the Web doubled in size every six months. It is estimated that it presently contains several hundred million pages full of information plus useful mechanisms for accessing it. And these pages are connected in a complex and arbitrary fashion as users continuously add links from their own pages to others that they think relate to their own information needs. As a result, a visitor to a page gets directed to other pages through a path that only reflects the idiosyncratic fashion with which the owners of pages relate to other information. Information feeds on information, sites have thousands of links, which in turn take the user to other pages connected to a myriad of other pages. And as this information changes, so do the links and the frequency with which certain sites are visited. This makes the Web into a veritable ecology of information, which is so rich in content that not even the best search engines can classify the ever growing number of pages.

This explosive growth has been accompanied by a large increase in the number of users of the Internet. Whereas in 1996 there were 61 million users, at the close of 1998 over 147 million people had Internet access worldwide. In the year 2000, the number of Internet users doubled again to 320 million.

In addition to its remarkable growth, the Web has popularized electronic commerce (e-commerce) and new types of electronic transactions, and as a result an ever increasing number of people conduct business in ways unheard of a few years ago. Chief among them are transactions involving intangible goods such as entertainment, travel, information, and banking services, as opposed to transactions in the traditional economy, made up of massive products such as computers and cars. Moreover, since e-commerce is conducted on a global scale, consumers can profit from increased knowledge of the products they purchase, lower transaction costs and prices, and a wider set of choices than those that are available in the traditional economy.

On the supply side, the Web offers providers access to global markets without having to incur large entry costs or to keep sizable inventories. This great opportunity is tempered by the increased competition that can result from newcomers continuing to offer novel combinations of products and ways of delivering them. The recent example of MP3, Napster, and the free distribution of recorded music over the Internet by nontraditional recording firms provides an illustration of the speed with which an industry needs to adapt to novel mechanisms and technologies in order to survive.

This adaptation will have to be swift, for the changes themselves are taking place at a very fast pace. Just as the music industry started to accept and perhaps incorporate the inevitability of MP3 into its own business plans, a new and even more threatening development took place with the appearance of Napster. This new system allows any owner of a computer to reach music stored in any computer partic- ipating in the system and to download it into her own com- puter. Basically a central directory of users and the music they have, Napster contains the IP addresses of all other computers willing to participate in a free-exchange system of music. So if someone needs to download a particular Bach cantata, for example, which he does not necessarily want to buy, all he needs to do is type the URL of Napster and spec- ify the piece of music that he wants. This action will connect him to a user who has the desired music so that it can be directly downloaded from the machine that has it onto the one that wants it. In a rather perverse way, Napster does not even have the illegally recorded music, just a directory of computers that have it, so it is not clear how illegal the ser- vice is.

By now it is clear that the phenomenon of the Web will eventually affect an increasing fraction of the world popula- tion and is bound to bring changes to the way we conceive of information, commerce, and communication with each other. Situated as we are in the midst of this explosion, it is too early to tell what the ultimate outcome of this revolution will be, just as it was hard to imagine the effects on society of the invention of radio, telephone, or cars.

Nevertheless, there are aspects to the current state of the Web that already reveal a lot about its growth, structure, and use. This is possible because of a certain kind of transparency that the Web offers, which translates into an ease of obtain- ing data about its structure and use that was unthinkable in the days of the industrial economy. In the past few years, a number of researchers have started to look into the way people access information, create sites, and communicate with one another via the ubiquitous browser. Others study the very structure of the Web, in terms of the number of pages it has, its links, and the ease with which one can move from one type of information to the other.

These studies have revealed a number of regularities that confirm our original notion of the Internet as an ecology of information. Moreover, the rules that describe the physical world are not the same as those operating in cyberspace, and part of my research has aimed at understanding how Internet users behave while they forage for information and engage in electronic commerce. The Web has become a veritable laboratory, where one can study human behavior with a precision and on a scale never possible before. These studies are closer to social science than computer technology, and they profit from the fact that the reach and structural complexity of the Web creates an ecology of knowledge. This ecology is characterized by relationships, information "food chains," and dynamic interactions that could soon become as rich as, if not richer than, many natural ecosystems.

The kinds of questions that we have been asking deal with the diverse strategies that people use to obtain information, or the formation of storms of activity that suddenly surge through the Internet, causing the short-lived delays we sometimes experience when downloading pages from a Web site. And why, just as mysteriously, do these Internet storms suddenly subside. Moreover, since the Web has a connectivity of its own, we try to determine how it grows, how interconnected it gets, and whether or not there are patterns to the number of pages or links a given site has.

These patterns turn out to be so ubiquitous that they can be considered as manifestations of underlying laws governing the growth of the Web and the way humans interact with it. In the following chapters, I describe these laws and their origin as well as show how their explanation in terms of the actions of individuals allows for novel and interesting ways of improving the use of the Web, both as an informational structure and a marketplace.

3   Evolution and Structure

Figure 3.1 (and in color on the jacket of this book), a seemingly random set of lines and dots, depicts an actual snapshot of a piece of the World Wide Web, corresponding to the collection of Web sites and links in Finland that existed about a year ago. This picture can be made a bit more intelligible by noting that the circles denote individual Web sites and the lines correspond to the links between them. But in a way this clarification is of little help. Any reader trying to make sense of this rather abstract-looking painting will eventually conclude, and rightly so, that this messy diagram, however appealing it appears, conveys little useful information besides its dubious artistry. It actually looks as if it were drawn randomly by some computer program or video game.

However, this apparently random figure contains a hidden and general pattern, found not only in the sector of the Web corresponding to Finland but everywhere else in the World Wide Web, from the United States to Europe or Asia. This hidden pattern, which I will discuss in this chapter, throws much light on the evolution of the Web and its structure. Equally important, its explanation and emergence as the Web grows relies on a powerful methodology that has turned out to be

Figure 3.1
Structure of the World Wide Web in Finland. The circles denote sites and the lines connecting them are links among them.

extremely useful in dealing with large distributed systems such as the Web.

This methodology aims to establish a tight relation between the local properties of large distributed systems and their global behaviors. Because of its analytical structure and its connection with observable properties of the Web, it has much predictive power. Examples of systems to which it can be applied are social organizations, markets, ecologies, and, most prominent, the Internet. In each case, the overall structure and dynamics of the system is determined by the collective interactions of its many autonomous parts, which include consumers, organisms, computer programs, or people. And because of the myriad interactions that are possible among the constituents of such large systems, the resulting behavior exhibits a panoply of complex and fascinating results that range from the apparent stability of large ecosystems to the wild fluctuations of financial markets.

The connection between the actions of individuals and the global patterns one observes is not always an obvious one, the reason being that the system behavior cannot be explained by simply adding up all the actions and intentions of its individual parts. If that were the case, it would be an easy task to add all the possible actions in order to predict the resulting behavior.

Systems whose behaviors cannot be explained by just adding all the partial actions of their constituents are known as nonlinear, and while they are more difficult to study than linear ones, understanding them is worth the increased effort. This is because the dynamics of nonlinear systems can be fascinatingly complex. For example, in addition to a simple equilibrium situation where the overall system does not change over time, or the textbook situations where patterns sharply repeat in clocklike cycles, nonlinear systems can also display erratic behavior even when their mathematical description is totally deterministic. In this so-called chaotic situation, if one were to start the system with a given condition and follow its evolution over time, the end result would be vastly different from what would follow if one were to start all over again from an almost identical initial condition. As a result, the behavior of systems that have this extreme sensitivity to their initial conditions appears to be extremely erratic, and the only predictions that can be made about their behavior are probabilistic in nature.

Nonlinearity is not the only complicating feature in the analysis of systems as complex as the Web. Its distributed nature also poses a formidable problem for its study. This is because the parts that make up the Web— sites, links added to them, or pages—can display complex nonlinear dynamics.

And when answers are found, their implications can be quite stunning, as they often imply an effective disconnection between the well-defined behavior of the components and the global outcome that one observes. What this means is that if one were looking at an economic system, for example, the precise knowledge about the plans and strategies of individuals in the market would not suffice to understand the behavior of a market. This important insight was first articulated by Frederick von Hayek (1937), when he stated that while economic outcomes are the result of actions by people, they do not necessarily reflect their intentions.

An example will help explain this important point. Consider an individual investor in the stock market of the day trader variety, and let's imagine that one can track all of his transactions in the market, as well as the messages that he exchanges with others. One might even imagine a rather implausible scenario in which one has access to his thoughts and deliberations on how and when to invest in particular stocks. If one were to do this for a very long time, one could end up learning whatever strategy this investor is using, and how successful it is for trading in the market. Even better, one might even get to know him so as to be able to predict with certainty his decisions in terms of buying or selling particular stocks. And while this imaginary scenario would teach one much about a given trader, it cannot predict the price of stocks in which he is about to make a decision. This is because the price of a stock depends on the behavior of many investors and their collective decisions—decisions that interact with each other in such complicated ways so as to drown out the effect of a single trader, who himself cannot anticipate the result of his own actions in determining the price of given stocks.

The example that I just described could be replaced with that of city traffic, where detailed knowledge of the driving patterns and intentions of a single driver cannot be used to predict congestion at an intersection, or to forecast which streets will facilitate traffic flow at given times. And the same applies to the characteristics of the Web, where detailed knowledge of how a given site grows by the addition of new pages and links to others is not enough to understand a picture like the one in figure 3.1.

Since following a single individual in her surfing behavior on the Web will not predict much about surfing in general, or how congestion takes place on the Internet, or the commercial success of given businesses, we must abandon such individual knowledge and replace it with something more aggregate, the behavior of the system as a whole. In order to do so, we developed methods for treating large distributed systems that are largely inspired by the success that physics has had with explaining the behavior of matter in terms of its constituents, such as atoms and molecules. These methods are statistical in nature and resort to dynamical formulations that lead to precise predictions that can then be tested experimentally.

This aggregate way of looking at a large system is a powerful methodology for dealing with large distributed systems, from stock markets to computer networks and social organizations. It provides a bridge between the particular and the whole, a way of reasoning that resorts to the dynamics of averages and the behavioral departures from these averages, while keeping the essential ingredients of what the component pieces do. It is thus possible to link the growth pattern of a given Web site to the total number of pages in the whole Web, or to make a connection between the individual intentions of users and the number of people who visit a search portal like Yahoo! in a week or a month. And so on.

The insights gained from this increased understanding of distributed systems when using knowledge about the behavior of their individual components has already led to improved methods for cooperative search algorithms, organizational design, and even distributed building controls. This gave me confidence that they would also be of use when applied to the Web, and indeed they did lead to the discovery of a number of strong regularities, such as the way the Web grows, how people surf it, the nature of markets in e-commerce, and how the act of downloading pages from a site contributes to the observed patterns of congestion.

How can we use this methodology to understand the growth patterns of the Web, which from its inception has demonstrated a tremendous variety in the size of its features? This variety is apparent to anyone who surfs the Web and anyone who notices the existence of large sites in terms of the number of pages they have, and also small ones consisting of one or two pages and few links to others. This is a natural reflection of the arbitrary way in which people design their own sites and decide what to link them to. A site belonging to a large firm, for example, might contain a lot of pages linked to each other and other sites, whereas that of an individual might have some biographical data, a picture, and one or two links to some of her friends.

Surprisingly, when one studies the structure of the Web on a large statistical basis, one finds out that in spite of the apparent arbitrariness of its growth clear patterns exist that reflect hidden regularities. One observed pattern is that there are many small elements contained within the Web, but few large ones. A few sites consist of millions of pages, but millions of sites only contain a handful of pages. Few pages contain millions of links, but many pages have one or two.

This diversity can be expressed in mathematical fashion as a distribution, a mathematical entity that quantifies how many instances of a given size, say, appear in the system one studies. The distributions describing the patterns observed on the Web have a particular form, called a power law. When we say that a distribution has a power law characteristic, we mean that the probability of finding a Web site with a given number of pages, n, is proportional to $1/n^\beta$, where β is a number greater than or equal to 1.

The interesting thing about a distribution with a power law form is that if a system obeys it, then it looks the same at all length scales. What this means is that if one were to look at the distribution of site sizes for one arbitrary range, say just sites that have between 10,000 and 20,000 pages, it would look the same as that for a different range, say from 10 to 100 pages. In other words, zooming in or out in the scale at which one studies the Web, one keeps obtaining the same result. It also means that if one can determine the distribution of pages per site for a range of pages, one can then predict what the distribution will be for another range of pages.

This power law distribution describes the number of pages per site, and also the number of links emanating from a site or coming to it. It is a robust empirical regularity found in all studies of the Web.

Figure 3.2 shows two examples of such power laws for the Web, which appear as straight lines because the scales are linear in each decade (or mathematically, logarithmic).

In figure 3.2, two power law distributions are shown: the distributions of the number of pages per site and those of links from one site to other sites (outlinks). Both look almost identical because both are power laws. If they were not, different shaped curves would result when plotted on scales that are linear in each decade.

Equally interesting is that power law distributions have very long tails, which means that there is a finite probability of finding sites that are extremely large compared to the

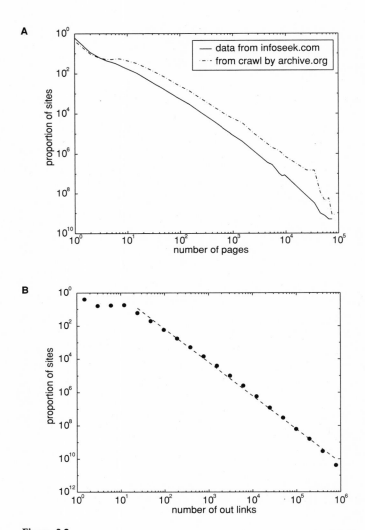

Figure 3.2
The proportion of Web sites having a given number of pages (A) and links
(B), plotted in logarithmic fashion.

average site. That this is quite striking can be illustrated by the heights of individuals, which we know follow the familiar bell-shaped normal distribution. The normal distribution determines, among other things, the average height of a person, which nowadays is about 5 feet 10 inches. Such a distribution is not a power law one, but rather it decays very fast for samples that depart from the average. Thus, one would find it very surprising to be walking in a city and to find someone measuring two or three times the average height of 5 feet 10 inches. On the other hand, when a distribution of some property, like the size of Web sites, has a power law distribution, it is it quite likely to find a site many times larger (in terms of the number of pages or links) than the average size.

Another peculiar consequence of a power law is that the average behavior of the system is not typical. A typical size is one that is encountered most frequently, while the average is the sum of all the sizes, divided by the number of sites. Thus, if one were to select a group of sites at random and count the number of pages in each one, the majority of the sites would have a smaller number of pages than the expected average. This discrepancy between average and typical behavior is due to the fact that a power law distribution, unlike the familiar bell-shaped one, is not symmetric around its maximum but skewed, and has a long tail.

The fact that the number of pages per site, and also the number of links per site, is distributed according to a power law is a universal feature of the Web. It holds throughout the World Wide Web, irrespective of the type of sites that one considers, from the smallest to the largest, and regardless of the nature of the site. The appearance of such a strong regularity out of a seemingly random process is quite striking, and points to some kind of universal mechanism that not only underlies the growth of the Web but also produces a power law distribution in some of its characteristics.

In order to describe this growth mechanism, consider first how pages are added to a site, say, a big site with a million pages. Such an enormous site must be maintained either by a very prolific author or by a team of webmasters continuously modifying, deleting, and adding pages. Equally possible, some pages on the site might be automatically generated. One would not be surprised to find that the large site of a million pages has lost or gained a few hundred pages on any given day. Now consider a site with just ten pages, a site that does not generate much content. Finding an additional hundred pages on this site within a day would be unusual—but not impossible. One could then safely say that the day-to-day fluctuations are proportional to the size of the site or, as it is stated in the mathematical description of this process, that the growth is multiplicative. In other words, the number of pages on the site, n, on a given day, is equal to the number of pages on that site on the previous day plus or minus a random fraction of n.

If a set of sites is allowed to grow with the same average growth rate but with individual random daily fluctuations in the number of pages added, after a sufficiently long period of time their sizes will be distributed according to a distribution that is known as lognormal. A lognormal distribution gives high probability to small sizes, and small—but significant— probability to very large sizes. But while skewed and with a long tail, the lognormal distribution is not a power law one, which is what one observes.

In order to explain the power law distribution of site sizes that one observes, one needs to consider two additional factors that determine the growth of the Web. The first one is that sites appear at different times, and the second is that some sites grow faster than others. A first scenario takes into account different start times. One knows that the number of Web sites has been growing exponentially since its inception, which means that there are many more young sites than older ones. Sites with the same growth rate appear at different times, only a few early on, but more and more as time goes on. After a sufficiently long time period, one finds a distribution that can be evaluated analytically and that has a power law behavior in the number of pages per site. The young sites, which haven't had much time to grow, are contributing to the low end of the distribution. The older sites, which are far fewer in number, are more likely have grown to large sizes, and contribute to the high end of the distribution.

In a second scenario, all sites appear at the same time, but their growth rates differ. By using computer simulations, we demonstrated that different growth rates, regardless of how they are distributed among the sites, result in a power law distribution of site sizes. The greater the difference in growth rates among sites the lower the exponent β, which means that the inequality in site sizes increases.

In summary, a simple assumption of random multiplicative growth, combined with the fact that sites appear at different times and/or grow at different rates, leads to an explanation of the power law behavior so prevalent on the Web.

The existence of this scale-free power law describing the number of pages per site for the whole Web is not only interesting but also useful. For example, a search engine that crawls the Web cannot know a priori how many pages per site it will encounter. If a program is written to stop downloading every page of a site beyond a certain number, this power law can tell, in a probabilistic sense, how many pages are left to crawl in that site. Another way of saying the same thing is to state that once a search engine crawls a large sample, knowledge of that distribution is enough to predict the rest of the crawl.

The distribution of the number of pages per site is not the only hidden regularity in the structure of the Web. As shown in figure 3.2, power law behavior is also observed when one studies the number of links per page, which were obtained from a crawl of 260,000 sites. By "site," I mean an address where each site is a separate domain name. If one counts how many links sites receive from other sites, as one found out for pages, the distribution of links among sites is power law. Equally interesting is the discovery that no correlation exists between the age of a site and the number of links it has.

This absence of a correlation between age and the number of links is hardly surprising, for all sites are not created equal. A site with very popular content, which appeared in 1999, will soon have more links than a bland site created in 1993. It is likely that the rate of acquisition of new links is proportional to the number of links the site has already. After all, the more links a site has, the more visible it becomes and the more new links it will get. This means that there the growth rate varies from site to site.

The theory that accounts for the power law distribution in the number of pages per site can also be applied to explain the number of links a site receives. In this model, at each time step the number of new links a site receives is a random fraction of the number of links the site already has. New sites appear at an exponential rate and each has a different growth rate, and when analyzed mathematically, this model explains the data well.

Before I continue, it is of interest to contrast these power laws with a similar kind of regularity that it is not only found on the Web, but in many other situations as well. This regularity goes under the name of Zipf's Law, in honor of George

Kingsley Zipf, a Harvard linguistics professor who sought to determine the frequency of use in English texts of the third or eighth or one-hundredth most common word. Zipf's Law states that the size of the rth largest occurrence of the event is inversely proportional to its rank, and so mathematically it looks very much like a power law. As a matter of fact, both power laws and Zipf's Law are used to describe phenomena where large events are rare, but small ones quite common. For example, few large earthquakes but many small ones occur. Few mega-cities but many small towns exist. A few words, such as "and" and "the," occur very frequently, but many occur rarely. And while there are a few multibillionaires, most people make only a modest income. Just as we found power law distributions in several properties of the Web, Zipf's Law also gives power laws but expresses them in terms of rank rather than numbers.

4   Small Worlds

It is a familiar experience to meet someone for the first time at a party, business meeting, or conference, and to soon discover that one shares an acquaintance or perhaps a family relationship that traces back to some common ancestor or distant uncle. The commonality of this case is the manifestation of a surprising and interesting social phenomenon, sometimes called "six degrees of separation," which holds that between any two people on this planet is a path of no more than six acquaintances linking one person to the other. While the exact number might not be six, it is the case that most often a short chain of acquaintances is all one needs to connect any two people chosen at random. This remarkable fact was discovered by Harvard sociologist Stanley Milgram who, in the 1960s, asked a number of randomly chosen people in a small town in the Midwest to mail a postcard to a friend of his, who happened to be a stockbroker living in Boston.

What made this experiment unusual was that rather than asking these people to mail the postcard directly to his friend, Milgram instructed them to send the cards by passing them from person to person, with the proviso that the cards should be passed to someone the passer knew on a first-name basis. Since it was highly unlikely that the initial group was acquainted with the Boston stockbroker on a first-name basis, they had to pass it on to someone that they felt would be closer to Milgram's friend either geographically or professionally.

Some of the cards eventually made their way to the target, and when Milgram analyzed the route they took he discovered that the average number of steps taken to get from the town in the Midwest to Boston was only about six, which shows that most people in a large population are connected by only a short chain of acquaintances. His finding was eventually confirmed in a number of careful social studies that range from friendships in high school to some religious communities. The generality of this result found its way into popular culture as plays and newspaper articles eventually highlighted the six degrees of separation phenomenon.

The phenomenon of six degrees of separation also inspired a number of games, such as Six Degrees of Kevin Bacon, where one attempts to find the shortest path from any actor to Kevin Bacon. Among mathematicians, authors of papers that are even distantly related to the work of the great Hungarian mathematician Paul Erdos carry a so-called Erdos number, which describes the distance to having co-authored a paper with him. Thus, for a mathematician to have an Erdos number of 1 means that he or she wrote a paper with Paul Erdos, while having an Erdos number of 2 implies having published a paper with someone who was a co-author of Erdos. What started as a game turned into a truth: The smaller the Erdos number, the higher the "prestige" felt by those who advertise it.

The existence of these so-called small worlds is not just a curiosity with possibly interesting mathematics behind it. It has practical and important consequences as well. Political influence, searching for a job, even the spread of diseases and other forms of social contagion, such as rumors or news, depend on the existence of such short chains of acquaintances, in ways that have been documented by social network scientists for over four decades.

In the context of the Internet this phenomenon can be readily explored on the Web at a site called <http://www.starwars.com/6degrees/>. Inspired by the phenomenon of six degrees of separation, it offers its users the possibility of discovering all sorts of small world connections among the characters and actors of the *Star Wars* movies.

Milgram's experiment raised two complementary and interesting issues (Milgram 1967). The first one had to do with the properties that networks must have to become small worlds. If one were to draw a network consisting of nodes that would represent people, and links among those nodes that would represent who knows whom, it is by no means obvious that any two nodes would be separated by six links. There is something particular about a social network that is reflected in the link structure of the network.

The second issue concerns what the best strategies are for navigating such small-world graphs in a short number of steps. The people participating in Milgram's experiment did not have detailed knowledge of the social network in which they were embedded, and yet they managed to pass the messages in a fairly short number of hops. Even knowledge of being part of a small world network does not necessarily translate into a smart strategy to deliver a message to a target person.

The first issue was partially addressed by Watts and Strogatz (1998), two mathematicians at Cornell University, and by researchers at Notre Dame University (Albert, Jeong, and Barabasi 1999). Watts and Strogatz created a procedure whereby a regular lattice can generate a small-world graph. Basically, they showed that a regular lattice can be transformed into a small-world network by making a small fraction of the connections random. But small-world networks are not just random graphs, since they have the property that they exhibit a high degree of clustering. This means that nodes are interconnected in such tight fashion that it would be unlikely to find such clustering in a random graph. By comparison, random graphs are not clustered and have short distances, while regular lattices tend to be clustered and have long distances.

One problem with this construction, however, is that these small word graphs lack an important property of many networks, namely, their approximate power law distribution in the number of links. This distribution amounts to stating that a few nodes or people or sites in the Web have many links whereas most have a few. Whereas some small-world graphs (for example, the electric power grid) are not power law–like, many are, such as the graph of who telephones whom. Such data can be obtained from the main telephone carriers.

Albert, Jeong, and Barabasi (1999), on the other hand, described a procedure for producing random graphs with a power law distribution in the number of links per node while failing to produce graphs that also have the clustering property of small worlds. While this work seems to explain the backbone structure of the Internet, it fails to account for the clustering property known to exist in the link structure of the Web. So, we are still in search of a proper understanding of small-world graphs that have a power law distribution in their link structure.

The issue of navigation in small-world graphs was also partially addressed by a computer scientist at Cornell University, John Kleinberg, who, starting with a perfect lattice, was able to construct a random graph with the right clustering properties. Unfortunately once again, the distribution of the number of links per node is not a power law, a fact that makes it irrelevant to those real-world problems where power laws are observed. The particular navigational algorithm that Kleinberg (2000) proposed has the property that a node has no knowledge of where the links from his neighbors go. While not leading to an optimal solution to the traversing of the shortest path between any two nodes, it does show the existence of fairly short paths for a particular value of the model parameters.

If the underlying mechanism for such small chains of connections among people reflects some mathematical property of random networks, and the Web is a good example of such a network, one may wonder if the same small world phenomenon exists among sites and pages, as opposed to people. Recently, Lada Adamic of the Xerox Palo Alto Research Center undertook a study of the average number of links that one has to traverse in order to go from one site of the Web to the other. Adamic (1999) found out that just as in the social sphere, one could pick two Web sites at random and get from one to the other within about four clicks. That this phenomenon constitutes a strong regularity of the Web was confirmed by looking at the link structure of a Web repository containing over 50 million pages and 260 thousand sites. Figure 4.1 exhibits this remarkable regularity in graphical fashion.

This phenomenon was also shown to exist for the number of links between any two pages, as opposed to sites of the Web, by researchers at Notre Dame University (Albert, Jeong, and Barabasi 1999). In this case the number is nineteen, as opposed to the four one encounters between sites.

The small-world phenomenon on the Web is not only interesting in itself but also useful, since it can be exploited in the design of better search engines and for the marketing of specific products in the world of electronic commerce. The reason for its usefulness lies in the common observation that a

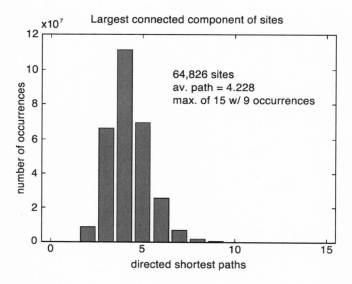

Figure 4.1
Histogram depicting the number of occurrences among sites having given directed shortest paths. From Adamic (1999).

good quality Web document tends to link to other good documents of similar content. Thus, one expects that within the Web there are groups of pages of similar content and perhaps quality, which refer to one another. The quality of these pages is guaranteed by the recommendations implicit in the links among them.

Adamic built an application of these ideas around a repository of Web pages crawled by the search engine Google in the first half on 1998. For any given search word, her application returned queries according to their page rank and their text match, while also providing link information for each page. It then identified all the connected clusters and selected the largest one, since most likely it is the one that contains links across sites besides the most common ones. What she noticed was that connected clusters spanning several sites tend to contain the main relevant pages and are rich in "hubs," or pages that contain links to many other good pages. One can then find the center of the cluster by computing the number of links among all the members of the cluster.

What this means is that rather than presenting a list of documents that contains many sequential entries from the same site, a search engine using the phenomenon of the small world can present just the center from each cluster, and then users can explore the rest of the cluster on their own.

The phenomenon of the small world on the Web has implications that go beyond the improvement of search engines. This is because the link structure of the Web implies the existence of communities that share some common affinities. The Web represents a wide range of human interests, and as a result some sites are devoted entirely to a single interest or cause. Others, such as Yahoo!, have clubs or chat rooms where people can meet and share their ideas on particular topics. Since many people document their interests and affiliations on their personal homepages, and link them to people with whom they have some common interests, the exploration of the link structure of documents on the Web can reveal the underlying relationship between people and organizations.

Recently, Lada Adamic and Eytan Adar realized that if both social networks and the Web were small-world graphs, then one would expect that networks of personal homepages would be small-world graphs as well. They confirmed this conjecture by studying the networks of personal homepages at two main universities in the United States.

By looking at listings of friends on the Stanford University and MIT homepages, they found out that users typically link to only one or two other users, with a very small but still significant fraction linking to dozens of users. This is yet another manifestation of the power law–like distributions discussed in chapter 3. In this case such power law implies that one finds some users with lots of links to others while most users have a few links to others. Some users are very popular, attracting lots of links, while most get only one or two. The more startling result that they uncovered is that users linking to only 2.5 other people on average create a virtual connected social network of 1,265 people and a few smaller networks. Furthermore, exploiting the notion that people who link to each other usually have something in common, they could predict who could be friends with whom by analyzing text, links, and mailing lists. Their methods show a lot of promise for discovering small-world communities of people by studying the way they link their pages.

5   As We Surf

Bookstores, particularly those offering a warm and inviting atmosphere, seem to have a special hold on many people. It is a common experience to drift into one's favorite bookstore and to browse books and magazines, drifting from one table or shelf to the other, connecting with topics close to one's interests, noticing new titles, sensing trends, or looking for news beyond that available at home. Whether one ends up buying a book or magazine is not that important; what matters is having spent a quiet time browsing and learning about the new offerings in print.

On reflection, this leisure browsing activity can appear quite mysterious and arbitrary to a curious observer, for if there is a pattern to it is by no means apparent. What makes us look at some books and not others? How long do we finger a book before moving to the next one? What makes us shift from one subject to the other, or what holds our attention to a particular page? Is it purely idiosyncratic, or is there a pattern that while different in its details applies to most people?

Move the focus away from bookstores onto the Web, and the browsing that I just described becomes replaced by the activity of clicking on page or site links that take the user from page to page within a site, or to new sites offering a dazzling diversity of content. This activity, surfing the Web, as it is called, can be studied in detail because it is relatively easy to record the surfing patterns of people using the Web. Since users can reach in a short time a staggering collection of documents placed in remote places of the world, unlike the bookstore example, moving from one section of the store to the other is now replaced with a simple click on a particular link. Moreover, one can keep track of usage patterns to a degree that is inconceivable in the real world of books and magazines. What the study of surfing reveals is not only a law that describes the way we hop from link to link, but also an interesting insight into human behavior and the existence of a kind of economy of attention that guides our surfing.

To understand surfing, one needs to consider how an individual goes about clicking on links as he or she surfs the Web. Imagine someone looking for a particular piece of information, putting a query to a search engine, and getting to a site that looks promising in terms of having the right answer. Once there, the user discovers a pointer or a link to something possibly unexpected but interesting. She clicks on the link and goes to a page that turns out to be perhaps surprising, with information that is relevant to the original query. This page is therefore valuable to the user, in the sense that she draws some utility from looking at it. Whether that utility is pleasure, time saved, or even money is irrelevant for our purposes. While reading this page, the user might discover a link to yet another page that promises to yield more information, or perhaps something closer to what she is looking for. Clicking on that link will bring the page, but not necessarily the value one assumed it had. The page might turn out to be different from what was expected, perhaps better, perhaps worse. If better, it might even lead to more interesting pages, and thus more surfing. Or, if useless, one may stop, go back, perhaps click on a link that one hopes will lead to better places to explore, or stop surfing all together. All that can be said is that the value of one page is related to the previous one by some quantity that seems to fluctuate from page to page.

It would seem from this description that surfing, mixing as it does impulses, curiosity, and user preferences, is not indicative of a general pattern. Worse, all that we said about this process so far is that because the value of the page about to be opened is not certain, it is only probabilistically related to the value one obtained when looking at the previous page. This is not something that one would call a predictive process. Worse, one can ask how much can be learned about something controlled by chance.

It turns out that the answer is surprisingly clear and predictive. Behavior of the type that I described, in spite of its probabilistic nature, takes place in a structured fashion. And the explanation for this structure also provides an insightful understanding of the surfing patterns of individuals while being able to predict the number of clicks that a typical user will make when accessing a site.

In order to see how it is possible to understand so much of a rather chancy process, it is worth describing how random phenomena first came to be deeply understood in a field far removed from the Web, that of physics at the beginning of twentieth century. In 1827, the botanist John Brown had noticed that when pollen particles suspended in a liquid were observed under the microscope, they displayed a wildly erratic behavior that seemed to be at odds with the predictable mechanics generated by the clockwise universe of Isaac Newton. The same phenomenon can be observed with small ink droplets suspended in water, or by looking at a light beam that enters a room through a window, casting a shiny path in which tiny particles appear to execute a random dance. This phenomenon, referred to as Brownian motion by scientists, remained a scientific puzzle until 1905 when Albert Einstein explained it by assuming that the tiny particles were being subjected to numerous collisions at random times with the molecules of the liquid in which they were suspended. His assumption was that while Newtonian mechanics was still operational on a scale of very short times, over long times the many collisions between the particle and the molecules of the liquid made the particle appear to have erratic behavior. A new type of dynamics had to be invented, a dynamics that dealt with random forces that only made sense over long periods of times, and in which only the average, long-term motion of particles mattered. By doing so, Einstein successfully described and predicted the motion of particles in a fluctuating environment. His work and that of his followers provided such an accurate description of Brownian motion that in 1925 the French physicist Jean-Baptiste Perrin was able to determine accurately the numerical value of a fundamental constant of nature from Brownian motion experiments.

An important consequence of the work on Brownian motion was the methodological shift that it implied for physical science. In one brilliant stroke, the deterministic description of nature best exemplified by the dynamics of planets and stars was suddenly enlarged and complemented with a different type of analysis, one that dealt with the *average* behavior of particles executing random motions as opposed to the exact wanderings of a single one. Just as one can speak of traffic on a road without being able to predict where a given car will go, so now can a physicist describe the behavior of random processes without having a detailed knowledge of all the forces acting on a Brownian particle. Moreover, this methodology is so powerful that even the departures from this average behavior provide useful information. That is the case with the scientific explanation for the flicker of starlight or the noise one hears on a radio channel.

One may wonder what Brownian motion and random walks have to do with surfing the Web, and the answer is that they are connected in an interesting and subtle fashion. Surfing involves not particles and forces, just people finding fluctuating value in the information they encounter. The value that a user gets at each click is randomly related to the previous one, for each time he gets to a new page, all that can be asserted is that its value to the user can only be connected to that of the previous page by some probability. And since an individual will stop surfing whenever the value found in this activity reaches a particular threshold, the number of clicks before stopping corresponds to the time it takes for a particle undergoing a random walk to hit a wall placed at a given distance from the starting point. If one knows that time, one can also determine the average number of clicks until an individual reaches a given threshold.

Since the values found by a user in the pages she visits while surfing constitute a random process, even a frequent user visiting the same site will go through a different number of clicks in every session. Thus, the only meaningful quantities to speak of are the average number of clicks per session, as opposed to the exact number that a person will go through at a particular time in a given day.

The number of pages that a user visits within a site is then determined by the probability that he or she will surf a given number of pages within a site. One can determine this probability by looking at the distribution of times it takes for a Brownian particle to hit a wall at a given distance from the starting point.

This distribution has a perfectly well defined mathematical expression, which can be plotted in a graph where the vertical axis has the values that the probability will take for a user clicking once, twice, and so forth, and the number of clicks is represented in the horizontal axis. Such a figure determines how far users will go clicking on the pages of a given site of the Web.

Figure 5.1, which indicates the probability that a user will go through so many pages when visiting a site, happens to give an accurate description of what actual users do. One knows this because in a number of very careful experiments Huberman et al. (1998) measured the surfing patterns of thousands of users making millions of requests from Web

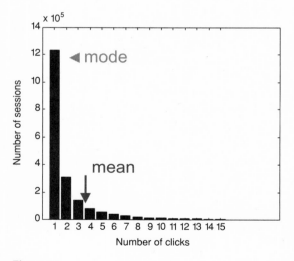

Figure 5.1
Users clicking on a given number of links within a site. The vertical axis denotes number of users and the horizontal one number of clicks. Notice that the maximum of the distribution (the mode), which determines typical behavior, is different from the mean, or average value.

sites. When the fraction of individuals surfing a given number of links is plotted as a function of the number of links clicked, one obtains a curve in good agreement with that predicted on the basis of the random walk argument.

So what else can be learned from this law of surfing? One thing to notice is that the figure showing the law of surfing has a skewed shape, resembling a distorted version of the familiar bell-shaped curve with one side having been squeezed against a wall. When a probability distribution is skewed, it means that rather odd events, like surfing a large number of pages during a given session, are quite probable. And yet, the peak of the curve, which happens to correspond to the most probable number of clicks a user would go through, is further down to the left, implying few page visits during a given session. This has an interesting implication for the way one computes the average number of clicks that a user goes through. This can be illustrated with the following example. Imagine a small village in a very poor country where a millionaire has decided to spend a year's vacation. If government officials were to take a census of people's income while he is there, they would compute an average much higher than before his arrival. And yet an unsuspecting tourist visiting the village a few years later would be hard-pressed to find in the streets people whose income corresponds to the average reported in the local statistics.

Just as resident millionaires of poor villages affect average income, users who surf many pages tend to generate an average number of clicks that is much higher than the typical number most users surf. This means that when dealing with statistics described by skewed distributions, as in surfing, the average conveys little information on surfing patterns.

Another interesting aspect of surfing is revealed by the fact that while the shape of the curve remains the same no matter what domain a user surfs, its peak and tail shift to the right or left depending on the nature of the domain. A recent study of the surfing patterns of more than half a million visitors to a portal site, conducted by Eytan Adar of Xerox PARC, showed that depending on the domain of inquiry, users indeed display unique surfing patterns, while still obeying the law of surfing. Schematically this is shown in figure 5.2, where each curve corresponds to the number of clicks that users make on different topics.

If each domain of inquiry corresponds to a different surfing curve, we can use this fact to improve the design of given Web sites, in particular those of portals, which are an important venue for e-commerce. Some important and popular examples are Yahoo!, Excite, and Lycos, to name a few. Portals attempt to act as a starting point for users on the Web and therefore lead consumers to e-commerce activities, such as travel and consumer electronics.

The business model of a typical portal service consists of two parts. The first is to have the consumer buy goods directly from the portal or through a partner site. The second

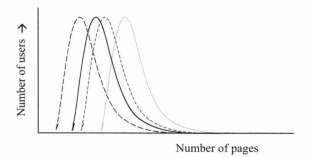

Number of pages

Figure 5.2
Surfing patterns for different domains of inquiry. Each curve corresponds to a different domain of inquiry.

part involves satisfying the user's information needs within the site and in the process presenting advertising banners that result in direct revenues to the portal. The mechanics of this approach are relatively simple. Users enter a portal site, search for information, see ads, and then leave.

While this model seems quite reasonable, further reflection reveals that it confronts the portal with a dilemma. Like any good business service, the portal strives to generate better and faster results for the users. However, if the results are presented at the entry point or at the first click into the site, leading users to another site, the user never travels deeply into the site, thus missing the advertising and consumer goods that he could potentially buy.

One solution to this problem, which has been adopted by many portal sites, resorts to the notion of stickiness, whereby providers attempt to keep consumers at their site by displaying potentially attractive links that point only to their site. An alternative solution could attempt to capture the existence of specific surfing patterns for given types of goods in order to solve this dilemma. This is similar in spirit to what is known in economics as consumer surplus, a notion that I will illustrate with a simple example.

Imagine having to prepare dinner for a number of friends that you have invited to your home and as part of the dinner you are baking an apple pie for dessert. You buy the apples at some supermarket near work and pay for them a price that basically reflects the ongoing supply and demand of apples in the neighborhood. A few hours later you are busy cooking the dinner when an accident happens and the glass pan in which you are baking the pie falls to the floor, destroying the pie. Bad news, but not necessarily catastrophic. Noticing that you still have a couple of hours before the guests arrive, you decide to bake yet another pie and you frantically start looking for apples in nearby stores. Now, given the urgency of the task, the price that you are willing to pay for those apples might be very different from what you paid earlier. The difference between what you are willing to pay and the ongoing price of apples at the supermarket is what constitutes consumer surplus. If store owners knew your sense of urgency and preferences, they could actually make more money for their products than what they do when charging a price that reflects a coarse-grained sense of demand.

In the case of surfing, the price one pays when visiting a portal is the time spent looking at pages. The owner of the Web site or portal could exploit the difference in surfing patterns among users searching for different kinds of information in order to increase the number of pages visited within a portal. One possible mechanism to accomplish this, which I developed together with Eytan Adar, goes under the name of "temporal discrimination." Since pages are linked to each other in many complicated ways within a site, it is clear that temporal discrimination provides multiple ways through which a user can reach the desired information. For each path there is an associated time that the user spends at the site, which depends on the number of links and the amount of time that each user spends at each page. In this context, time becomes a proxy for the price a consumer pays to access the information.

This process is illustrated in figure 5.3. The graph illustrates a basic Web site structure. Each circular node represents a Web page, and each line a directed connection between nodes. A user usually enters the site from the start (home) page. In this example, the target is the black node. The time a user takes to reach the target is a function of various things, including structure and expertise. More interesting for our purposes is that the number of clicks will also be a function of the amount of time a user is able to spend in reaching the

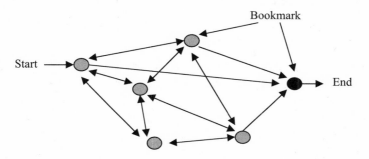

Figure 5.3
The structure of a basic Web site. Each circular node represents a Web page, and each edge a directed connection between nodes. A user usually enters the site from the homepage (left node). In this example, the target is the black node. The time a user takes to reach the target is a function of various things, including structure and expertise.

target. A user can get to the goal in one step or, because of ignorance about the site organization, through several links, thus making it costlier to access the desired information.

Alternatively, a user may store a link pointer as a bookmark, in which case he can access the desired page without having to navigate. This means that different users are willing to pay different prices (in terms of time) for the same informational good.

If users are willing to pay different prices for the same good, one should be able to construct demand curves in the time domain that would show different users going through different number of clicks when accessing the same source of information. Figure 5.4 shows this by depicting the amount of time (in number of clicks) that users are willing to spend for a given service need, given the link structure of the information provided by the site. Analyzing the surfing patterns of over half a million visitors to a popular site produced this data, which reflects the fact that there is a law of surfing

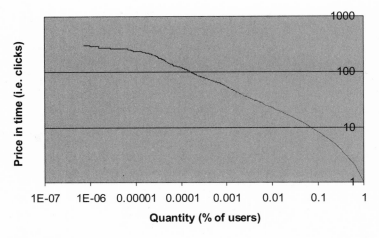

Figure 5.4
Aggregate demand curve for a www portal. The vertical axis corresponds to
the number of clicks (which amounts to price in time) and the horizontal axis
depicts the fraction of users performing that number of clicks.

determining the probability that users will surf through a
given number of clicks.

The point to notice is that if demandlike curves like this
exist for any kind of information needed, when information
providers satisfy consumer needs at a fixed number of clicks
they are missing the additional time that some users are willing to spend in order to get that same information.

Several strategies can be employed to extract maximum
surf depths from consumers exploring a portal or e-commerce
provider. The first one is a general procedure that works with
any commercial Web site, whereas the second is ideally suited
for information providers, such as search engines and shopping directories.

An obvious first strategy consists of constructing a Web
site that changes its link structure to lengthen the path tra-

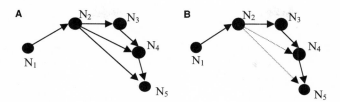

Figure 5.5
(A) Schematic arrangements of links for a Web site with various pages (large circles) connected by various directed links. (B) Same as in (A) with the links from node 2 to 4 and 5 switched on or off.

versed by a given user, thereby making him visit many more pages. For example, if a short route (in the number of clicks) exists to a given page, one may wish to turn that off if the user is statistically likely to visit more pages in between. An example of such dynamic organization is described in figure 5.5.

Notice that a user entering page 1 has only two choices: entering page 2 or leaving the site. At page 2, a user now has three choices. If one can predict with some degree of certainty whether or not the user's trajectory will pass through pages 4 or 5, and there is a user willingness to continue clicking further, one can remove the direct links from page 2 to pages 4 and 5.

The second strategy relies directly on the existence of the law of surfing, which determines the number of users who will surf to a given depth within a site. The basic scheme consists in collecting surfing data for each site for a fixed level of quality of service. The data would then have the shapes shown in figure 5.2. The typical number of links a user will surf, which is given by the maximum of the curve, determines when to provide the good-quality information or the incentives to go to other pages.

In order to extract the surplus indicated by the shifted maxima in the curves, one can offer a second version of the service with different quality characteristics. This new version can be integrated into the service along with decision rules—trained by the usage logs—that decide which version should be offered to the user. Thus, users can now continue to surf using this new version and therefore spend more time in a given provider's site.

These are just a few examples of the many ways knowledge providers employ a strong regularity in the way users surf the Web to extract a maximum value from them.

6   Social Dilemmas and Internet Congestion

Consider a scenario that will be familiar to many people. You and a group of your friends go out to dinner at a nice restaurant. All of you are of fairly equal means, so there is the unspoken agreement that the check will be divided evenly at the end. What do you order? Do you choose the chicken entrée or the pricey lamb chops? The glass of house wine or the 1983 Cabernet Sauvignon? A few dollars extra divided by the size of the group won't affect your wallet much, but if everyone reasons the same way as you, the group will end up with a hefty bill to pay. But if they don't, you'll have enjoyed a superlative dinner below cost. The flip side is that those with moderate tastes and appetites have to pay for their more extravagant companions. Why settle for pasta primavera when everyone else is having grilled pheasant at your expense?

There is another aspect of this group dinner to consider. It may be that this same group of friends goes out together every week. So, even if you do not keep track of who was extravagant and who wasn't, you still have a pretty good idea of what your share came out to be the previous week, and that reminds you of roughly how many of your friends chose to free ride by ordering an expensive entree and how many "cooperated" by choosing a cheaper one. This in turn affects your decision as to whether or not you show restraint next time, especially if you keep in mind the mounting tab as the week progresses.

The humor in this example, named the Unscrupulous Diners' Dilemma in an article published in *Scientific American* (Glance and Huberman 1994), belies the seriousness of the issue. The dilemma faced by the diners is representative of a class of problems that are pervasive in society and difficult to resolve. Environmental pollution, arms races among traditional enemies, population explosion, conservation of electricity and fuel, and giving to charity are just a few examples of situations where an individual benefits by not contributing to the common cause. But if all individuals shirk, everyone is worse off.

An interesting example of this social dilemma appears in the context of using the Web. Because Internet users tend to pay a flat fee for access to it, the Internet is a public good and its millions of users are not charged in proportion to their use. It therefore appears rational for individuals to consume bandwidth greedily while thinking that their actions have little effect on the overall performance of the Internet. Because every individual can reason this way, the whole Internet's performance can deteriorate considerably, which makes everyone worse off. And yet, from a single individual's perspective, to restrain from downloading a page from a Web site in order to decongest the Internet does not seem like a very rational strategy.

Since they were first made explicit, these dilemmas have attracted the attention of sociologists, economists, and political scientists, for they are central to issues that range from securing ongoing cooperation in volunteer organizations such as unions and environmental groups to the possibility of having a workable society without a government. Although no simple solutions to social dilemmas exist, their study sheds light on the nature of interactions among people and the emergence of social compacts. And because such dilemmas involve the interplay of individual actions and global behavior, they throw light onto a fundamental problem that lies at the root of social phenomena. The problem is how to relate the actions of a group of individuals whose personal choices are known in some detail to the impressive diversity of social outcomes to which they can give rise.

One way to study social dilemmas is to conduct controlled experiments in which a group of people are given a set of choices that present an inherent conflict between the global good and the costs to an individual. A number of such experiments have been performed, and many confirm the hypothesis, first made by the economist Mancur Olson in the 1950s, that smaller groups are more likely to secure voluntary cooperation than larger ones. These experiments are typically conducted with university students, and they are designed in such a way that each individual is given the choice to either cooperate by participating in some group effort, and thus share in the total earnings of the group, or defect and get the earnings without putting any effort into the outcome. Of course, the catch is that if all members of the group choose to defect, no one gets anything. Experiments of this kind also reveal specific conditions that tend to encourage cooperation among participants. For example, they established that repeated iterations of the same situation tend to promote cooperative attitudes. Interesting as they are, these experiments have been criticized for not representing real life situations, since they are conducted in laboratory settings where individuals are given a simple choice between two actions, cooperate or defect, while ignoring all sorts of complicating factors that are present in everyday life.

The study of congestion on the Internet provides yet another way to observe social dilemmas, but this time without many of the simplifications of laboratory experiments. In this case, the characteristics of the network are such that in spite of the large number of users, the equilibrium state is cooperative, or, in other words, most of the time the bandwidth available satisfies the needs of most surfers. Like consumers of a natural resource such as clean air, or drivers during rush hour, surfers are faced with a social dilemma of the type exemplified by the well-known "tragedy of the commons." The social scientist Garret Hardin first articulated this tragedy of the commons (Hardin 1968), and he did so by considering an area of farmland, the commons, entirely owned by a group of farmers who graze their sheep there. In this situation, it is in the farmers' best interest to maintain herds of moderate size in order to keep the pasture from being overgrazed. However, it is in the best interest of each farmer to increase the size of his herd as much as possible, because the shared pasture is a free resource.

Even worse, although each herdsman will recognize that he should forgo increases in the size of his herd if he is acting for the good of the group, he also recognizes that every other farmer has the same incentives to increase the size of his herd as well. In this scenario, each individual has it in his individual interest to take as much of the common resources as he can, in part because he can benefit himself and in part because if he doesn't someone else will, even though doing so produces a bad outcome for the group as a whole.

Bandwidth utilization on the Internet is also a commons problem, and it manifests itself in many ways, two of which I discuss in this chapter. The first one has to do with congestion and the time it takes to download pages from the Web, whereas the second manifestation of this commons problem appears in the functioning of peer-to-peer distributed systems like Gnutella.

Consider the problem of congestion. Because Internet users are not charged in proportion to their use, it often appears rational for them to consume bandwidth greedily while thinking that their actions have little effect on the overall performance of the network. Because every individual can reason this way, the whole Internet's performance can deteriorate considerably, which makes everyone worse off. But as users experience a congested network, they reduce or even desist in their use, freeing up bandwidth that can once again be consumed, and so on. Current technology makes it quite easy to observe and measure this behavior, and thus offers the opportunity to study the unfolding of a social dilemma in a natural setting. Equally interesting, the precision with which one can measure behavior in this setting provides new and interesting insights into cooperation and into the nature of congestion in computer networks.

Mathematical theories of social dynamics describe the observed effects and make predictions that can be validated empirically, and as such they provide a complementary way to study social dilemmas. Theories of social dilemmas have been formulated by economists and political scientists within the framework of game theory, a discipline that was developed in the mid-1940s by the mathematician John von Neumann and the economist Oskar Morgenstern to provide models for the behavior of individuals in economic and adversarial situations. Game theory relies on a number of underlying assumptions that provide a rough approximation to how people really behave. One is that an individual's choices can be ranked according to some payoff function. The payoff function assigns a numerical value to each choice: its equivalent worth in dollars or apples, for example. Another is that individuals behave rationally, which in game-theoretic language means that they choose the action that yields the highest payoff. While it is debatable as to whether or not people consistently make rational choices, rationality is known to direct behavior when people are presented with simple choices and straightforward situations. Witness, for example, the behavior of players in the tic-tac-toe game. Once they learn the rules, they choose their moves in such a way that to an outside observer they appear completely rational.

Social dilemmas of the type exemplified by the Unscrupulous Diners' scenario can be readily mapped into a game-theoretic setting. In this case, the common good is achieved by minimizing the common bad: the amount of the check. "Cooperating" means choosing a less expensive meal; "defecting" is sparing no expense (for the group that is!). Of course, the mapping isn't perfect, since the game is an idealized mathematical model while the Unscrupulous Diners' Dilemma is a real-life situation. For suppose that the payoff function is defined as the enjoyment of the meal (which is hard to measure in dollars) minus the cost of the meal. This would leave out many variables such as peer pressure and personal ethics, which are extremely difficult to quantify.

In the case of Web surfers, the mapping to a game-theoretic setting is accomplished by realizing that what users try to maximize is the speed with which they access remote information. They can be considered cooperators if they show restraint in their use of the Web, or defectors if they consume bandwidth greedily. Now, users don't usually think of themselves as cooperators or defectors. They stop downloading a page because of long delays without much thought to the cooperative nature of their actions, but from a game-theoretic perspective they act as such, since they effectively reduce congestion when they stop surfing. The more people desist from surfing, the faster the bits travel through the Internet. Therefore, in the case of the Web, collective benefits increase with the number of cooperators, at some rate per cooperating member. In the context of the Internet, this rate is proportional to the speed with which remote sites can be accessed, a quantity that exhibits fluctuations over many time scales. On the other hand, each cooperating individual incurs a personal cost that reflects the penalty paid for delaying access to the information that he or she needs.

As millions of users engage in this dance of downloading pages, stopping when the system gets slow and starting up again when bandwidth becomes plentiful, the level of congestion on the Internet goes up and down accordingly, reflecting the dynamics of the underlying social dilemma. And since surfers do not communicate with one another or even know what others are doing, one would expect that congestion would fluctuate wildly, like static on the radio.

But when Lukose and I (Huberman and Lukose 1997) looked in detail at the fluctuations in congestion that would result from the unfolding of a social dilemma, we discovered that the emerging pattern was quite different from that of radio static. Rather, what emerges is that although most of the time the available bandwidth is not completely taken up by greedy behavior, the network's behavior is punctuated by sudden spikes of congestion, sometimes called Internet "storms," which quickly subside as slowdowns become intolerable and users reduce or end their surfing. Moreover, we demonstrated that these intermittent spikes in congestion are not distributed according to the familiar bell-shaped Normal distribution, but in a very skewed fashion, meaning that most of the time congestion is low and every once in a while a large peak in congestion take place. What is surprising about these Internet storms is that they imply a large degree of coordination among surfers who are not even aware of the existence of each other. This is because for a short, intense burst of congestion to occur, many people must start using the Internet at the same time and decide to quit surfing in almost synchronized fashion. This implicit coordination is the result of the social dilemma, whose signature then appears in the form of these Internet storms.

We (Huberman and Lukose 1997) tested these predictions by conducting two types of experiments. The first one consisted of measuring the round-trip time it takes for computer signals to go to another computer and return to the sender. This is accomplished by sending packets of information from one computer to another around the world and measuring how long it takes for them to get there and return to the originating computer. By sending thousands of packets to many computers all over the world many times during the day, Huberman and Lukose were able to determine how many packets took a given amount of time to complete their round-trip. If this data is plotted in such a way that one ends up looking at how many packets took so many milliseconds to execute a round-trip, one obtains the distribution of travel times that is a statistical measure of congestion on the Internet. When Huberman and Lukose did so, the plots revealed that congestion, which affects the travel time of these packets, was distributed according to the theoretical prediction. That is, the probability that one observes a given level of congestion was given by a skewed distribution with a long tail.

The second experiment involved trying to download a number of pages from remote sites on the Web and measuring how long it took for them to arrive at the requesting machine. Once again, we (Huberman and Lukose 1997) measured the same distribution that we obtained when measuring the round-trip time of packets.

How is it that one is able to predict the existence of Internet storms starting from the general setting of a social dilemma? While a detailed answered is mathematical in nature, one can describe the basic ingredients of the theory without having to resort to any equations. First, one needs to specify the set of beliefs that surfers have when downloading pages and encountering delays. These are quite simple to state. Users monitor the level of utility and, if latencies are noticeable, they stop surfing, expecting that if they do so the network will be less congested in the future. Obviously if the information one needs is very important or urgent, one pays a price when deciding to obtain it later. In the words of game theory, users decide to switch their behavior between cooperation and defection by considering the cost of postponing their current activity as well as their expectations of the future state of the network. Specifically, users who experience congestion tend to believe that others do so as well and expect that if they try again later, the network is likely to be less congested. Similarly, users who experience little congestion will tend to take advantage of it and consume as much bandwidth as they require. Thus, because users believe that other users behave similarly to them, they expect that if the network is heavily congested now, it will be faster later.

Several years ago, together with Natalie Glance, I looked at the dynamics of social dilemmas facing people with these kind of expectations, as well as others, and found out there exists a collective group strategy of conditional cooperation that maximizes utility for the members of the group (see Huberman and Glance 1997). The strategy can be simply stated. A surfer will cooperate if the utility that she is greater than a critical fraction and defect if it is less. Basically this amounts to a threshold condition, which if satisfied leads to one type of behavior, and if not to another.

Even when all surfers use this conditional strategy, there is always the occasional fluctuation away from equilibrium whereby individuals might switch over short periods of time from nonuse or restrained use to heavy use, and vice versa. These switches are due to different levels of need and impatience in obtaining information, to the uncertainty that individuals have about the congestion of the network, and to random changes in the environment of the Internet. Each of these uncertainties can cause an individual to mistakenly perceive the total amount of Internet use to be different from its actual value. Because of this misperception, the user might then act against the equilibrium condition, causing the system to move away from the fixed point. The more uncertainty there is in the system, the more likely it is that there will be fluctuations away from the equilibrium state.

When fluctuations in the levels of restraint take place, the group recovers in time according to an equation that governs the dynamics of fluctuations away from the equilibrium state. The solutions to this equation show that typical fluctuations away from overall restraint relax back exponentially fast to the equilibrium point. On the hand, there is the remarkable result that the average number of defecting individuals increases over time. This indicates that the behavior of the system is dominated by occasional large bursts in which the number of individuals suddenly found not to be refraining from Internet use is very large, leading to spikes of congestion characteristic of Internet storms. We encountered this difference between typical and average behavior earlier in the context of the law of surfing. Typically, one still finds most citizens making much less than the average. In the context of the Internet, the notion of an average download time is thus not very useful for characterizing the level of congestion on the Web.

The fact that average and typical behavior are different in the case of Internet traffic also leads to a cautionary note when speaking about the average performance of the Internet. As I said in chapter 5, having a single millionaire move into the town can raise the average income of the population of a given town, but it does not mean that its citizens are wealthier because of it. Thus, data such as that provided by several directory services, which is averaged over thousands of sites, can be misleading if used to predict levels of congestion. Rather, a typical Internet user would encounter latencies shorter than those indicated by average behavior.

Finally, the existence of a law of congestion is not only interesting because of the light it throws on the dynamics of social dilemmas, but also helpful in the design of algorithms for speeding up traffic on the Internet. This is the subject of chapter 7.

I now discuss a second manifestation of the social dilemma in the context of the Internet. It is a topical one that concerns the sudden appearance of new forms of network applications such as Napster, Gnutella, and FreeNet. These networks, made prominent in the media because of issues of copyright infringement and the threat they pose to established music production houses, hold a lot of promise for the emergence of fully distributed information sharing systems. This is because these so-called peer-to-peer systems will allow users worldwide access and provision of information while enjoying a level of privacy not possible in the present client-server architecture of the Web.

While a lot of attention has been focused on the issue of free access to music and the violation of copyright laws through these systems, there remains the additional problem of securing enough cooperation in such large and anonymous systems so they become truly useful. Since users are not monitored as to who makes their files available to the rest of the network (produces) or who downloads remote files (consumes), nor are statistics maintained, the possibility exists that as the user community in such networks gets large, users will stop producing and only consume. This free-riding behavior is once again the result of a social dilemma that all users of such systems confront, even though they may not be aware of its existence.

As we already discussed, in a general social dilemma, a group of people attempts to produce and utilize a common good in the absence of central authority. In the case of a system like Gnutella, the common good is the provision of a very large library of files, music, and other documents to the user community. Another common good might be the shared bandwidth in the system. The dilemma for each individual is then either to contribute to the common good, or to shirk and free ride on the work of others.

Since files on Gnutella are treated like a public good and the users are not charged in proportion to their use, it appears rational for people to download music files without contributing by making their own files accessible to other users. Because every individual can reason this way and free ride on the efforts of others, the whole system's performance can deteriorate considerably, which makes everyone worse off—the tragedy of the digital commons.

The second problem caused by free riding is that it can create vulnerabilities for a system in which there is risk to individuals. "Risk" in this context means being identified as a user of the system in situations when an individual might want to remain anonymous. If only a few individuals contribute to the public good, these few peers effectively act as centralized server. Users in such an environment thus become vulnerable to lawsuits, denial of service attacks, and potential loss of privacy. This is relevant in light of the fact that systems such as Gnutella, Napster, and FreeNet are depicted as a means for individuals to rally around certain community goals and to "hide" among others with the same goals. These may include providing a forum for free speech, changing copyright laws, and providing privacy to individuals.

Given these concerns, Eytan Adar and I decided to conduct a set of experiments to determine the amount of free riding present in the Gnutella system. These experiments revealed that a large proportion of the user population, upwards of 70 percent, enjoy the benefits of the system without contributing to its content (Adar and Huberman 2000).

If distributed systems such as Gnutella rely on voluntary cooperation, this rampant free riding may eventually render them useless, as few individuals will contribute anything that is new and of high quality. Thus, the current debate over copyright might become a nonissue when compared to the possible collapse of such systems. This collapse can happen because of two factors: the tragedy of the digital commons and increased system vulnerability.

Individuals participating in the Gnutella network can contribute in two ways. The first is simply by uploading files, thus making them available to the rest of the user population. The second is by actively participating in the protocol of the network, thus providing the "glue" that holds the network together. It may be then that all peers on the network contribute even if they provide no downloadable files. However, there is a point at which peers that act only as glue provide diminishing returns to the system, leading to at least two ways in which the quality of the service deteriorates.

First, peers who provide files are set to handle only a limited number of connections for file downloading. This limit can essentially be considered a bandwidth limitation of the hosts. Now imagine that there are only a few hosts who provide responses to most file requests. As the connections to these peers is limited they will rapidly become saturated and remain so, thus preventing the bulk of the population from retrieving content from them.

A second way in which quality of service suffers is through the impact of additional hosts on the *search horizon*. The search horizon is the farthest set of host machines reachable by a search request. For example, with a time-to-live of five, search messages will reach at most peers who are five hops away. Any host that is six hops away is unreachable and therefore outside the horizon. As the number of peers in Gnutella increases, more and more hosts are pushed outside the search horizon and files held by those hosts become beyond reach.

One argument that has appeared in the popular press regarding systems such as Gnutella is that there is a diminished risk of the system being shut down because of either lawsuit or attack. It will be impossible, users argue, for the recording industry to sue all of them. This belief, which was spread by the press, allowed users to believe that they were safe among others and therefore free to use the system. Unfortunately, in light of the evidence provided, Gnutella provides a false sense of security.

As I pointed out, the experiments revealed that there is a small collection of peers who provide the bulk of the shared files and answered queries. These few providers act as a rather centralized server consisting of several peers, and thus the recording industry need not sue all users or even the bulk of users. They simply need to target the top-serving peers (of which there are very few that serve very many).

So, how does one overcome free riding?

Many ways exist of patching Gnutella so that it can accommodate the same privacy rules but scale more effectively. It is interesting therefore to establish how different file-sharing applications rely on technological features to induce users to share. FreeNet, for example, forces caching of downloaded files in various hosts. This allows for replication of data in the network forcing those who are on the network to provide shared files. Unfortunately, such a system is prone to replication of "bad" or illegal data and "tainted" hosts. The second cost of the automatic replication as implemented in FreeNet is the unique identifiers for files that forces users to know exactly what they are looking for.

Napster, by default, downloads all files into a shared upload directory. In this way, when a user downloads a file it is automatically shared. In some ways this feature addresses the FreeNet problem because users will only keep "good" files on their computers. However, users can easily circumvent this shared upload/download directory and frequently do. Both systems provide their own set of solutions to the free riding but at the cost of introducing other problems to their systems.

Another possible solution to this problem is the transformation of what is effectively a public good into a private one. This can be accomplished by setting up a market-based architecture that allows peers to buy and sell computer processing resources, much in the spirit in which Spawn was created. In this context, one should stress that the utility to users does not necessarily have to be monetary. For instance, issues of prestige or status drive participation in open source systems like Linux, and the same can be said of SETI, where obviously to be the owner of the PC that detects the first intelligent signal from outer space would constitute great utility.

Another alternative for eliminating free riding is to reduce the cost to the users of such systems. For example, the Usenet system, while allowing some degree of anonymity, provided a great advantage to individual users as their messages were distributed by an infrastructure that offloaded the bandwidth requirements for individuals. That is, the only cost to the user was the initial posting; afterward the message was propagated by the system.

7   Downloading Information

A few months ago, the daily news that is routinely brought to me by my homepage in my Web browser contained an interesting story. A sophisticated and expensive space probe that NASA had sent to Mars lost contact with its tracking stations due to an error in converting rocket pressure from the English system of units to the decimal system. Intrigued by such a blunder, I decided to check it out by going to the NASA Web site. I clicked on the link to NASA only to discover that nothing was happening. How could it, when thousands of people were interested in the same story and were trying to download the same page. This was congestion of a higher degree than the one just discussed. Not only was the Internet being flooded with pages from NASA, but presumably even the servers in Pasadena had trouble handling all the traffic into that site. I waited for about ten seconds and, frustrated, I pressed the Stop button to cancel the request for the page. After a few seconds, I pressed the Reload button and, to my surprise, the page appeared almost instantaneously. All it took was stopping and restarting again, and as if by magic the hard-to-get Web page was suddenly on my screen.

Anyone who has ever browsed the World Wide Web has probably encountered the same phenomenon and used a similar strategy, which works most of the time. Click on a link, wait a few seconds, and if nothing happens, stop and reload again. If congestion were constant, this would make no sense, but as we saw in the chapter 6, congestion on the Internet happens in bursts. As a result, the time it takes for pages or packets to travel the same distance between any two computers has a wide variability. Sometimes a whole page will travel from the server to the user in a very short time, and at other times the same page will take a long time to get through the same set of Internet routers to its destination. Thus, when we press the Reload button and get the page almost instantaneously, we are essentially riding among congestion spikes in such a way that the contents of the page are able to travel from the client to the server in a time interval between congestion bursts.

As most surfers have noticed, this large variability in travel times is not always bad, since it can be used for speeding up the downloading of Web pages. But other implications of this variability exist that are not as useful or even as harmless. Take, for example, the case of foreign currency traders operating over the Internet. Since these electronic transactions also involve the exchange of packets of information between computers, they do exhibit a wide range of completion. This can be a serious impediment if the underlying price of the item being traded changes fast. One would not like to be in a situation whereby one presses the Enter button to buy or sell something at a price posted on one's screen, only to have it change by the time the order arrives at the client machine. In the age of the Web, when the medium of communication and negotiation becomes a distributed network of computers equipped with robust, secure, and trusted "cash" mechanisms, it is extremely important to reduce the variability in travel time for electronic transactions.

Most of the current proposals for managing congestion on the Internet and reducing the large variability in communication time stress the need to develop some form of usage-based pricing. It is therefore likely, if not inevitable, that in the future users will be charged for transmitting the information necessary to complete commercial transactions. Such costs would be analogous to the cost of postage when sending a bill by ordinary mail, or to the cost of maintaining Automatic Teller Machines (ATMs) in order to deliver cash to bank depositors, or to highway tolls, and so forth.

For an institution like a bank, with high transaction volume, new and potentially comprehensive delivery channels such as the Internet raise important issues of how to manage efficiently the costs and any risks associated with them. Just as banks have tried to encourage the use of ATMs in order to cuts costs and have set up contingency plans in case unforeseen problems affect the physical delivery of important materials such as checks, so will banks have to consider various options in order to manage the cost and risk involved in completing electronic transactions. However, assuming the existence of a comprehensive electronic delivery channel, the range of possible risks and costs that need attention is considerably reduced, since issues such as the mechanical wear in ATMs are not relevant. In fact, it might well be that the time it takes to complete a transaction will be the most important parameter that needs to be optimized in any e-commerce transaction, representing in essence the whole cost of the transaction.

But as we saw earlier, while time to complete a single transaction is one thing, variance also plays a role. In financial terms, one can actually consider the variance in the transaction time to be the risk associated with the transaction, since it tells us how likely it is that a given piece of information will depart from its average travel time. This risk is especially important for a high-volume institution such as a bank, which has to coordinate many different transactions for a given user. These transaction may depend on one another in complicated ways and proceed in a given order.

What one needs therefore are mechanisms that reduce both the typical travel time between any two computers and its variability. We saw a rather primitive and manual way of doing this when downloading Web pages and pressing the Restart button. While doing this manually is not very practical for e-commerce, it suggests the implementation of a similar and automated strategy for any transaction on the Internet, be it in the form of a bank engaging in currency trades or a search engine having to "crawl" the Web. The idea is to have an optimal time at which to restart the page request or to resend the information in such a way that both the time it takes for the page to download and its variability are significantly reduced. I now outline such a strategy, based on ideas from the field of financial economics, which was jointly developed with Rajan Lukose and Sebastian Maurer while they were at the Xerox Palo Alto Research Center (see Maurer and Huberman 2001).

The basic idea behind an automated reload mechanism is borrowed from portfolio theory. In modern portfolio theory, the fact that investors are risk-averse means that they may prefer to hold assets from which they expect a lower return if they are compensated for the lower return with a lower level of risk exposure. Equally interesting, it is a nontrivial result of portfolio theory that simple diversification can yield portfolios of assets that have both higher expected return as well as lower risk. Similarly, in the case of e-commerce, we can consider different methods of executing transactions as analogous to asset diversification, and as yielding mixed strategies that allow an efficient trade-off between the average time a transaction will take, and the variance or risk in that time. As in the case of financial portfolios, we designed a set of restart strategies in such a way that they can execute transactions faster on average and with a smaller variance in their speed than what one obtains without this strategy.

In order to explain how this technique works, let us first look at the download time for the main page of over 40,000 Web sites. This is exhibited in figure 7.1, where the vertical axis displays the number of pages downloaded, and the horizontal axis denotes the time it took to download them. As can be

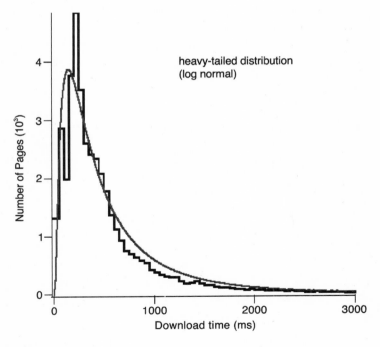

Figure 7.1
Distribution of downloading time for randomly selected Web pages. The smooth curve corresponds to the lognormal distribution.

seen by focusing the attention on the maximum height of the curve, which determines the typical behavior, one concludes that most pages arrived within 250 thousandths of a second. The fact that the distribution has a long tail also means that some pages took a much longer time to arrive at the computer. Thus the strategy that one needs to design would hopefully make the maximum height of the curve move toward the left (shorter download times) and become narrower, meaning a much smaller variance in download times. In the case of latencies on the Internet, thinking of different restart strategies is analogous to asset diversification: there is an efficient trade-off between the average time a request will take and the variance or risk in that time.

Consider a situation in which a message has been sent and no acknowledgment has been received for some time. This time can be very long in cases where the latency distribution has a long tail, as is the case in figure 7.1. One is then faced with one of these choices: continue to wait for the acknowledgment; send out another message; or, if the network protocols allow, cancel the original message before sending out another. For simplicity, I discuss the case when it is possible to cancel the original message before sending out another one at a particular restart time. Since a fluctuating network is being considered, one can only speak of the probability that the page will download within the given restart time. Similarly, the probability exists that it will take longer than the restart time to arrive. From this probability, one can compute the average time that it would take someone to download a page. Since that average will change as the restart time is changed, it becomes a function of the restart time. One can also compute the variance around the average download time, which indicates how likely it is that pushing the Restart button at the given restart time will cause the page to download within that average time.

The details of this calculation can be found in the original research findings (Maurer and Huberman 2001). What matters here is that these calculations take into account the law of congestion discussed earlier, which determines how download times are distributed over time. When these calculations for the average and variance in download times are performed, and the results are plotted as a function that has as its vertical axis the average download time and as its horizontal axis the variance, one obtains a curve where each point corresponds to a different restart time. This is why we speak of a "portfolio" of restart times. For each value of the restart time, one obtains an average or expected download time and a variance. The full curve for the range of possible restart times is shown in figure 7.2. Even a cursory look will convince the reader that it indicates the existence of an optimal strategy, suggested by the extreme point where the two branches of the curve meet.

Why is this point optimal? Because for this particular value of the restart time, both the variance in arrival time and the time it takes on average to download the page are minimal. There is no other value of the restart time that can improve on this result, for any other value would take us on other parts of the curve that are above the optimal point.

This portfolio method can then be implemented automatically by measuring the distribution of download times for a set of Web pages, or the time it takes for packets to go from one computer to another. From this distribution one then constructs a portfolio curve like the one shown in figure 7.2, and easily determines the optimal restart time, which can then be programmed into the browser or the machine performing crawls.

One potential problem that the reader will quickly identify lies in the possibility that everyone will start using this strategy,

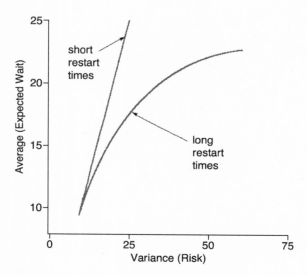

Figure 7.2
A portfolio of restart times for downloading pages from the Web. The horizontal axis denotes the variance in downloading times, whereas the vertical
axis shows the expected waiting times. As the frequency with which the
Restart button is pushed increases, one moves from the upper-right end of
the curve downward toward the minimum and then upward on the left
branch of the curve.

thereby congesting the network with all these restart requests,
in which case its benefits may actually be lower than when a
single user implements it. Since everyone reading this book
by now has learned about this strategy, we are once again confronted with yet another example of a social dilemma. Should
one desist from using the portfolio strategy so that congestion
is lower for everybody? What if one desists, but everybody
else does not, creating a situation where one is worse off than
most? Or should one use it in hopes that others do not?

There are two ways to answer this question, and both
involve trade-offs. One could try an experiment with several

thousand of users who decide whether or not they want to use the portfolio strategy. This is a very hard thing to implement and measure, since to determine the resulting congestion one would have to sort it out from other sources of congestion. Or, in a simpler and cleaner approach, one can perform computer simulations of this scenario and decide on the basis of the results whether or not it pays to use the method. But the problem with this is that computer simulations can never incorporate all the decisions that individuals can make when confronted with such dilemmas.

Nevertheless, the use of computer simulations in the study of social interactions is extremely useful when trying to determine the effects that changes in the behavior of individuals have on the dynamics of the group as a whole. It is usually difficult to test hypotheses within, say, an organization, without creating disruptions and producing unintended results.

Computer simulations also allow scientists to test hypotheses without incurring the cost of implementing experimental policies whose results are unknown. Equally important, if done properly and with simple agents, a computer simulation can quickly provide a sense of whether or not certain assumptions will result in the expected behavior. Finally, an important consideration is that the unfolding of the social dynamics in a simulation takes place in times that are much shorter than any social experiment, thus allowing for the testing of complex scenarios in a timely fashion. A social experiment might take weeks or months to complete, and its analysis might be so involved that one might have to retry it several times before deciding on its outcome.

In order to see the effects of the social dilemma implied by the use of a portfolio method by all surfers, Sebastian Maurer of the Xerox Palo Alto Research Center performed a series of computer simulations of a group of agents deciding asynchronously whether or not to use the Internet (see Maurer and Huberman 2001). The agents based their decisions on knowledge of the congestion statistics over a past window of time. As I showed in chapter 6, such a collective action dilemma leads to an optimal strategy, which is basically determined by a threshold function: cooperate if parameters of the problem are such that a critical function exceeds a certain value, and defect otherwise. In terms of the dilemma posed by using the Internet, this translates into downloading pages if latencies are below a certain value and not doing so if they exceed a particular value.

Thus, in the simulations each agent is restricted to a simple binary decision, and the dynamics are those of a simple threshold model with uncertainties built in. With this in mind, we modeled each agent as follows: an agent measures the current congestion, expressed in arbitrary "waiting time" or units. Since the waiting time is a function of the number of users, and their number fluctuates in time, it is reasonable to make the decision to use or not use the restart strategy a function of the load over a past window of time. This load is used to calculate the perceived waiting time using different strategies, which amount to deciding when to resend the request. The agent then compares the perceived waiting time to a threshold: if the former is larger, he decides to cooperate and refrains from using the Internet. If the waiting is short enough, he decides to defect and uses it. Agents make these decisions in an asynchronous fashion, meaning that they do not all act at the same time, since it would lead to all sorts of artifacts in the simulation.

The results of the computer simulations were both revealing and interesting. It turned out that when every agent uses a portfolio strategy in order to deal with Internet congestion, one can still find a portfolio for each of them and such that all agents are better off using it than not. Even when all agents use the optimum restart strategy, the situation is no worse than when no one uses the restart strategy.

What this means is that the use of a portfolio strategy in trying to reduce the variability of electronic transactions, and the speed with which they take place, will lead to beneficial results even when many users implement it. In reality, this strategy will not be used by millions of users at precisely the same time, and therefore their effects on others will be further reduced.

A final anecdote illustrates the power of these ideas in influencing professional lives. When Sebastian Maurer performed these experiments, he was a doctoral graduate student in physics interested in studying the dynamics of the Internet. By the time he graduated, writing a thesis that contained these results, he had decided to leave physics and the Internet behind and became a financial analyst for an investment company. So it goes with portfolios.

8 Markets and the Web

It is almost impossible nowadays to open a newspaper without encountering a story about e-commerce. The early euphoria about the new Information Age and the companies that helped people forage for information has been replaced by tales of millions of dollars traded in minutes over the Internet, from online booksellers like Amazon to the country-wide garage sale conducted by eBay. And this is just the tip of the iceberg; business-to-business e-commerce keeps growing at a phenomenal pace.

The news stories, while at times a bit exaggerated, reflect an explosive reality. If there is a word to describe the emerging digital economy it is "surprise." Even the experts continue to underestimate the potential of e-commerce. A recent report by the U.S. Department of Commerce reveals that in 1997 most forecasts predicted that the value of Internet retailing could reach $7 billion by the year 2000. And yet this number was already surpassed by 50 percent in 1998. In 1999, several studies of e-commerce tripled their previous estimates of the near-term growth expected in business-to-business e-commerce. By opening an immediate and convenient channel for communicating, exchanging, and selecting information, business-to-business transactions are also allowing firms to reconsider those functions they should perform "in-house" and which are best provided by others. For example, a firm might discover that a particular manufacturing process can be outsourced to another company that can produce the same parts faster and cheaper than would be possible inside the original firm.

The new technology is also helping to create new relationships and to streamline and augment supply-chain processes. It might be that forecasters are indeed underestimating the power of the Internet, but most likely we are witnessing a situation where it is not even known which quantities to measure in order to understand the growth of e-commerce.

In spite of the transformational wave that e-commerce represents, it is important to keep some perspective on its phenomenal growth. First, one should remember that a large fraction of the world's population still lacks access to water or electricity, let alone computers to engage in information foraging or e-commerce. Second, even in the United States, as a share of the retail portion of the economy, e-commerce remains quite small—less than 1 percent as of mid-1999. On the other hand, the same report by the U.S. Department of Commerce shows that the producers of the infrastructure that underlies e-commerce—the computer and communications hardware, software, and services—do play a significant strategic role in the growth of the U.S. economy. Between 1995 and 1998, these information technology producers, while accounting for only about 8 percent of the U.S. gross domestic product (GDP), contributed on average 35 percent of the nation's real economic growth. Equally important, their prices kept falling during the period 1996–1997, which contributed to the remarkable ability of the U.S. economy to control inflation and keep interest rates low in a time of historically low unemployment. It is reasonable to expect that this trend will continue, not only in the United States but in Europe and Asia as well.

From an economic standpoint, the growth of e-commerce seems to promise the advent of an era when markets will be frictionless. By frictionless, I mean a situation characterized by strong price competition, ease of search for best values, and low margins for the producers. How close we are to that frictionless market in the realm of e-commerce is a matter of debate, but the indications are that e-commerce is increasing the efficiency with which many transactions are performed.

A number of studies about the nature of e-commerce do point to an increasingly efficient digital economy. These studies, which have been recently summarized by a group at the Sloan School of Business at MIT (Brynjolfsson and Kahin 2000), have concentrated on price levels, their elasticity, menu costs, and price dispersion in a number of digital markets. To study price levels on the Web amounts to asking whether or not prices charged on the Internet are lower than those charged in standard outlets. Several studies of books and CDs sold through conventional and Internet outlets first showed that that these goods traded at higher prices in the digital world than in the physical one, but a newer study conducted a year later revealed that the situation had reversed.

Other researchers have looked at demand elasticity in electronic markets, that is to say, whether or not consumers are more sensitive to small price changes than consumers in the physical economy. For commodities, price elasticity is an important characteristic of an efficient market. In this arena, the findings are not consensual, and they range from the discovery that price sensitivity is lower online than in conventional outlets to the fact the provision of better product information over the Web actually softens price competition while increasing the fit between the consumer and her needs.

Another question to ask of digital markets concerns the frequency and fine-tuning with which e-commerce retailers adjust their prices; do they do so more finely and more frequently than retailers in, say, a shopping mall? Two recent studies (see Brynjolffson and Kahin 2000) show that the answer is indeed affirmative; with Internet retailers making price changes that can be a hundred times smaller than the smallest ones in physical outlets.

Finally, price dispersion addresses the question of whether or not there is a smaller spread between the highest and the lowest prices that people have to pay for the same good on the Internet versus at an ordinary outlet. Although the characteristics of the Web would make one expect a lower dispersion online than in conventional markets, recent studies do not support this hypothesis. Several reasons have been articulated to explain this finding, such as the fact that retailers resort to market segmentation strategies, or even price discrimination, charging different amounts of money depending on the quantity of the product being purchased.

It is therefore safe to conclude that the digital economy seems to be displaying a tendency toward frictionless markets that will become more pronounced as more suppliers and buyers enter this medium, provided of course that governments keep their regulations to a minimum.

The point of view that I have articulated in this book suggests that it is now time to ask whether or not one observes strong regularities in the commercial transactions that take place on the Web. The conditions seem to be there: a large number of commercial sites and consumers, and access to data. Given all the ferment and growth around e-commerce, it is natural to look for patterns in the buying and selling activities of millions of consumers who use the Web.

Recently, together with Lada Adamic, I looked at the issue of market share on the Web, which determines the proportion of sites that capture the attention of the population that uses the Web (see Huberman and Adamic 1999). We did so by examining usage patterns of Internet providers, covering hundreds of thousands of sites. In this context, users acted as proxies for economic activity, in the sense that visits to a site were used as a crude gauge of their economic success. This is not as unreasonable as it may seem, for even when nothing is ever purchased, sites make money from advertising and subscriptions whose remunerability depends on the number of visitors per day that they get.

We first obtained the distribution of users among sites from access logs of a subset of America Online (AOL) users on a given day. The subset comprised 60,000 users accessing 120,000 sites. A request for the document such as <http://www.b.com/c/d.html> was interpreted as a request for the site b.com. This definition of a site was chosen for lack of information about individual site content. Sites b1.com and b2.com might comprise a single conceptual site but were counted separately. Furthermore, visits to multiple documents within the same site or multiple visits to the same document were counted only once. Thus we related the popularity of a site to the number of unique visitors it received in one day. Table 8.1 shows the percentage of volume (measured in unique visitors) accounted for by the top sites.

As can be seen, the top 0.1 percent sites, excluding AOL itself, capture a whopping 32.36 percent of user volume. The top 1 percent of sites captures more than half the total volume, with yahoo.com dominating in terms of visits.

To control for difference in kind and function of sites, we also looked for unequal distribution of volume within categories of sites that we expected to have similar content. The

Table 8.1
Distribution of user volume among sites in general, adult sites, and .edu domain sites, as determined by counting the number of unique AOL visitors on Dec. 1, 1997.

% Volume by User	% sites		
	All Sites	Adult Sites	.edu Domain Sites
0.1	32.36	1.4	2.81
1	55.63	15.83	23.76
5	74.81	41.75	59.50
10	82.26	59.29	74.48
50	94.92	90.76	96.88

two categories we chose were adult and educational domain sites. Adult sites were assumed to offer a selection of images and optional video and chat. Educational domain sites were assumed to contain information about academics and research as well as personal homepages of students, staff, and faculty, which could cover any range of human interest. Again, the distribution of visits among sites was unequal. 6,615 adult sites were sampled by keywords in their name. The top site captured 1.4 percent of the volume to adult sites, while the top 10 percent accounted for almost 60 percent of the volume. Similarly, of the .edu sites, the top site (umich.edu) held 2.81 percent of the volume, while the top 5 percent accounted for almost 60 percent of all visitor traffic.

When we analyzed the data, we found that both for all sites and for sites in specific categories, like sex, travel, or education, the distribution of visitors per site follows a universal power law similar to that found earlier in the distribution of pages per site or links per page. This result implies that a newly established site will, with high probability, join the ranks of sites that attract just a handful of visitors a day, while with an extremely low probability it will capture a significant number of users. This is not a very optimistic message for those dreaming of becoming rich overnight by starting a new Web site.

This finding implies that a small number of sites command the traffic of a large segment of the Web population, a signature of winner-take-all markets. These winner-take-all markets, characterized in detail by the economist Robert Frank (Frank and Cook 1995), are characterized by having the awards given in proportion not to the absolute performance of a given business with respect to the others, but to its relative standing with respect to others. This is a familiar situation in sports, entertainment, and management circles, where a famous athlete, actor, or CEO commands a phenomenal salary compared with that of a second- or third-best athlete. This situation exists in spite of the fact that most often the difference in their performance is so small as to make it imperceptible to most observers.

Here are two simple but compelling examples. A few singers dominate the world of opera and make most of the money, whereas those with slightly less perfection in their voice or personal charisma have to live on the incomes provided by private lessons and small concerts, not likely to result in vast sums of money. The same applies to famous movie stars appearing in films with others who, although similar in their acting abilities, get much smaller fees than the star.

This finding is surprising because if standard economic theory were to apply, one would expect that being marginally less good would translate into a small difference in income for the actors or singers with slightly different abilities, since people would tend to pay a price for their performance that would reflect their true, or absolute, standing and not how they compare to others.

In order to explain this market law, one needs a dynamical theory of site popularity that takes into account the fact that user decisions to visit given sites appear to be made at random, as well as the fact that newer sites are appearing on the Web at an ever increasing rate. The model that we developed accounts for the observed power law behavior and naturally provides the amplification factor responsible for the increased performance of the top performers (Huberman and Adamic 1999).

Here is a thumbnail sketch of the theory, which will also serve as a reminder of the methodology used to explain the distribution of pages per Web site that I explained in chapter 3.

First consider the number of users frequenting a given site as a function of time. A large site with thousands of users might fluctuate by hundreds of visits on any given day, whereas a small site with dozens of users might experience a few visits more or less. This means that the difference in the number of visitors at a site in two successive time periods is proportional to the total number of users. In other words, the day-to-day fluctuations in the number of visitors to a site is proportional to the number of visitors the site receives on average. Moreover, visitors belong to essentially two classes. In the first category are those who are aware of the site, and who may or may not return to the site on this given day. A fraction of them does return, and this fraction varies from day to day. Hence the changes in the number of visitors are multiplicative—that is, proportional to the number of visitors on the previous day.

Those who are visiting the site for the first time or rediscovering it after some time has elapsed define the second category of visitors. Those in the first category who are familiar with the site influence the number of new visitors. The influence can be direct—one person telling or e-mailing another about a cool site he has have just discovered, or one he uses regularly. It can also be indirect, for a person that discovers an interesting site might put a link to it on her homepage, which in turn can act as a pointer for others to find it. A site with many users can get media coverage, which brings in even more traffic, with a consequent increase in the number of links from other sites. Finally, the amount of advertising a site can afford to pay to attract additional users depends on the amount of revenue it is generating, and this revenue in turn depends on the number of visitors. Hence the number of new visitors to the site is also proportional to the number of visitors on the previous day.

Once again, to understand the dynamics of site visits, one needs to incorporate the fact that sites appear at different times and have different growth rates. Some grow quickly because they deal with a topic that is of interest to lots of people, others because they provide quality of service, and still others because influential sites link to them. Some sites may grow quickly because they bring in their clientele from the physical world, while others start on the Internet but advertise heavily both on- and off-line. Some gather their entire user base purely through customer loyalty and word-of-mouth advertising. When all these factors are put together, one obtains a distribution in the number of visitors per site, which once again is power law as observed. In other words, the probability that a site has n visitors is proportional to $1/n^\beta$ where the exponent β is a number close to 2.0.

One possible consequence of this theory is that the oldest sites might be the dominant ones in terms of attracting the most visitors. But interestingly enough, the measurements show that site popularity and age are only slightly correlated. For example, the seventh most popular adult site was only created four months prior to our measurements—fairly young, even by Web standards. Clearly, assuming the same growth rate for all sites is an insufficient factor in the theory, and hence we need to take into account differences in the mean and variance of the increase in popularity of Web sites, since so far the distribution is valid for a single growth rate.

Many factors can affect a site's growth rate, including name recognition, advertising budgets and strategies, usefulness and entertainment value of the site, and ease with which new users can discover the site, to name a few.

The implication of this result is interesting both to the economists studying the efficiency of markets in electronic commerce and to providers contemplating the number of customers the business will attract. Remember that if the distribution of visitors per site follows a universal power law, it implies that a small number of sites command the traffic of a large segment of the Web population. A newly established site will, with high probability, join the ranks of sites that attract a handful of visitors a day, while with an extremely low probability it will capture a significant number of users.

These results lead a number of people to feel disappointed with the nature of the Web, as it would seem to contradict its "democratic" nature. But the winner-take-all nature of these markets does not necessarily imply a lack of commercial fairness. Several points can be made about this.

The first one has to do with the democratic nature of the Web. While it does not take an immense investment and a large infrastructure to establish a new commercial Web site, equality of opportunity does not imply equality of outcome. As we saw in our discussion of the power law distribution, a number of factors make it unreasonable for sites with relatively similar content to expect a fair share of the market. The vast size of the Web makes it hard for single individuals to find the best sites, and they rely on a mechanism of social search to optimize their findings without spending undue amounts of time searching for the best providers. Second, since many providers lack recognizable reputations and can offer similar services, it is seldom possible to make optimal decisions about which sites to use and which ones to avoid. If the consumer has never heard of a given provider, how sure is she that the service purchased will satisfy the quality that the consumer expects to receive?

The solution to this problem, which has been around for a long time in our more familiar physical space, is now starting to appear in cyberspace as well. When confused by similar offerings, customers rely on the value of a brand name in order to choose. Brands are essentially a short encoding of a number of attributes that belong to a firm or a set of products, such as their quality, their price, and the history and reputation of the firm offering them. The value of a brand can be so high as to surpass the tangible assets of a firm. Such was the case when several German car manufacturers recently decided to bid large amounts of money in order to buy Rolls Royce of Britain. What was at stake was not an efficient manufacturing technology or a large distribution network, but the association that most people make between quality and prestige when thinking of Rolls Royce.

The value of a brand can also be so low as to lead to decreasing revenue streams and eventual bankruptcy. Witness the case of ValuJet Airlines, which after the catastrophic accident of Flight 592 in 1996 went downward in the public's perception and eventually merged with AirTran Airways in order to be able to draw customers unaware of the name change. These two extreme cases are examples of the value that a brand can bring to a firm. It can actually be quantified in real dollars in spite of the fact that it extends beyond the tangible assets of a firm. When someone considers buying a company, the price that the potential buyer is willing to pay in excess of the tangible assets is called good-will accounting, and it basically defines the brand-name value of the firm.

In the case of the Internet, branding solves the problem of the vast anonymity that pervades cyberspace. Any provider of consumer goods or information on the Web appears to be no more than an attractive-looking Web page displaying lists of products and prices. What is hard to judge from that description is the quality of the offerings. Consumers are thus confronted with a problem: how does one trust the offerings of a Web site, and how does one judge the quality of its service without any prior experience with this particular business?

It is here that brand name plays an important role, leading to the expectation that if the brand is well known, one would obtain service that one has experienced earlier in a different setting and locale. Witness the phenomenon of McDonald's or Coca-Cola, which basically consists in assuring hungry or thirsty people traveling anywhere in the United States or abroad of the same consistent level of quality and service, irrespective of the city or country where the product is delivered.

In cyberspace the problem is not consistency among disparate geographical regions but spotty quality and unreliable service from e-commerce sites. This is why brands such as Yahoo!.com and Amazon.com eventually become synonymous over time with a level of quality and reliability that gets delivered consistently. And yet, how can all the others, the vast majority of e-business firms in cyberspace with no brand-name recognition, engage in profitable relations over the Internet?

One possible solution to this problem relies on third parties to act as certification centers for many service providers whose brand name is not recognizable to the consumers. These electronic intermediaries can serve both as certifiers of particular commerce sites and as recommenders when queries from consumers arrive at a search site. In many cases, companies with an established brand name in cyberspace could also become branding entities. Such was the case when Amazon.com announced the appearance on its site of links to pharmaceutical products provided by a company that it now partially owns. While Amazon as a company had little to do with pharmaceuticals, its reputation in selling books on-line carried enough clout so as to engender trust in consumers looking for pharmaceutical products. One can envision many other services, such as accounting, billing, and so forth, to become certified by other well-known companies or intermediaries so that people will be able to engage in reliable commerce with them.

Another subtle form of branding is the appearance of links in a given Web site pointing to other sites. Such links act as an implicit recommendation to a Web user to go visit another site. It could be the result of a paid-for advertisement, or some other arrangement that the commercial provider has with the alternative site. In either case, the fact that such a link originates with a site that one trusts is enough for the consumer to increase his sense that the new site might be more reliable than a totally unknown one found at random. These links are a form of umbrella branding, for they seem to imply an endorsement of a site or products by a company whose brand name might have better recognition.

Epilogue

As I hope to have shown in this book, there is order in the midst of the gargantuan and arbitrary nature of the Web. And this order can be explained by using reasonable and simple assumptions about human behavior in the context of the Internet. The mathematical methods used to discover this order might be technical, but the ideas flow from insights into the behavior of individuals to the result of their myriad interactions. From the evolution of the Web with its small beginnings in Switzerland to the nature of markets mediated by this new medium, I have shown that strong and sometimes beautiful patterns emerge, and that those patterns in turn reveal a lot about social dynamics, individual preferences, and order beyond the appearance of total disorder.

While the Web is the topic of this book, many of the underlying explanations and even the kinds of laws described hold for other informational structures—everything from visits to bookstores to markets in the brick-and-mortar realm. But what I have tried to stress here is that the existence of the Internet leads to qualitatively different phenomena if only because of the scale at which they can be studied. These laws and explanations are not about a group of people being observed while they shop on-line or communicate with one another. Rather, I have been observing and explaining the behavior of a vast, diverse population of millions of people, scattered throughout the world and leaving traces of their surfing and Web site building efforts that offer insightful clues to human behavior.

In a sense, I have only scratched the surface of what these studies can reveal. In the next few years, we'll see increasingly sophisticated tools deployed to explore and exploit such useful and vast knowledge about human behavior. And in this exploration, many issues that have not been discussed in this book will end up becoming central to the development of the new information-based economy.

First and foremost among these issues will be the one dealing with privacy concerns that have been surfacing since the very inception of the Web. The capacity to personalize offerings and to study the surfing and shopping patterns of countless individuals can also work in a perverse way to monitor them, expose them, and even blackmail them, if necessary. While in the United States a rather libertarian approach has been the dominant mode until now—one in which individuals and companies, rather than the government, are left to sort out these potential threats—Europe has chosen from the beginning to put into effect laws that protect individuals from the improper use of the data that is collected about them. While this latter approach might appeal to some, it creates barriers for the exchange of information that leads to more efficient markets. Given this gap in the management of privacy across the Atlantic, I suspect that one will see efforts to reconcile and perhaps converge using these two approaches. Within Europe, individuals who will perceive the advantages of giving away some privacy in exchange for cheaper loans, and better and more focused advertisements might try to push their governments into a looser control of privacy issues, while in the

United States the opposite might become true. It would take a few well-publicized cases of gross privacy violations for the public to start putting pressure on their legislators to issue regulations along the lines of the European model.

Big issues loom concerning the applicability of national and regional laws to cyberspace, and in particular the resolution of commercial conflicts between consumers in one country and providers in other. The very recent edict of the French government forbidding Yahoo! from displaying any auction items containing Nazi paraphernalia, and the consequent fight in U.S. courts against that injunction by Yahoo! shows how complex these issues can become. On the other hand, a historical precedent exists in the way multinational corporations are subject to local and international laws, and that precedent could extend to the Web. If this is the case, those very liberating aspects of the Internet that were responsible for its explosive development might fade away. That will leave us with something less exciting, less spontaneous, and less creative than what we've seen so far.

It is too early to tell, because one should not dismiss the fascinating interplay between new laws and their enforcement, and the ingenuity of those who can always device novel ways of bypassing those restrictions. Witness the example of Napster, quickly complemented with peer-to-peer systems like Gnutella when threatened by lawsuits and attempts to close it down. The incentive will always be there to offer new mechanisms for which laws will be created and for which technological and legal loopholes will always be found. As more and more people rely on the Internet, more creativity is bound to be unleashed, which will in turn provide new challenges to institutions and governments, who will then react only to be challenged again. O brave new world!

References

Adar, E., and B. A. Huberman. 2000. Free riding on Gnutella. *First Monday* (October). Available at <http://www.firstmonday.dk>.

Adamic, L. 1999. The small world Web. In *Proceedings of the 3rd European Conference on Digital Libraries.* Lecture notes in Computer Science, 443–452. New York: Springer.

Albert, R., H. Jeong, and A. Barabasi. 1999. The diameter of the World Wide Web. *Nature* 401: 130.

Brynjolffson, E., and B. Kahin. 2000. *Understanding the Digital Economy.* Cambridge, Mass.: MIT Press.

Frank, R. H., and P. J. Cook. 1995. *The Winner-Take-All Society.* New York: Free Press.

Glance, N. S., and B. A. Huberman. 1994. Dynamics of social dilemmas. *Scientific American* (March): 76–81.

Hardin, G. 1968. The tragedy of the commons. *Science* 162: 1243.

Hayek, F. A. 1937. Economics and knowledge. *Economics* 4: 33–54.

Huberman, B. A., and L. A. Adamic. 1999. Growth dynamics of the World Wide Web. *Nature* 401: 131.

Huberman, B. A., and N. S. Glance. 1997. Beliefs and expectations. In *Modeling Rational and Moral Agents,* ed. P. Danielson, 211–236. New York: Oxford University Press.

Huberman, B. A., and R. Lukose. 1997. Social dilemmas and Internet congestion. *Science* 277: 535.

Huberman, B. A., P. Pirolli, J. Pitkow, and R. Lukose. 1998. Strong regularities in World Wide Web surfing. *Science* 280: 95.

Kleinberg, J. 2000. Navigation in a small world. *Nature* 406: 845.

Maurer, S. M., and B. A. Huberman. 2001. Restart strategies and Internet congestion. *Journal of Economic Dynamics and Control* 25: 641.

Milgram, S. 1967. The small world problem. *Psychology Today* 1: 61.

Shapiro, C., and H. R. Varian. 1999. *Information Rules: A Strategic Guide to the New Economy*. Cambridge: Harvard Business School Press.

Watts, D., and S. Strogatz. 1998. Collective dynamics of small-world networks. *Nature* 383: 440.

Zipf, G. K. 1949. *Human Behavior and the Principle of Least Effort*. N. Reading, Mass.: Addison-Wesley.

Index